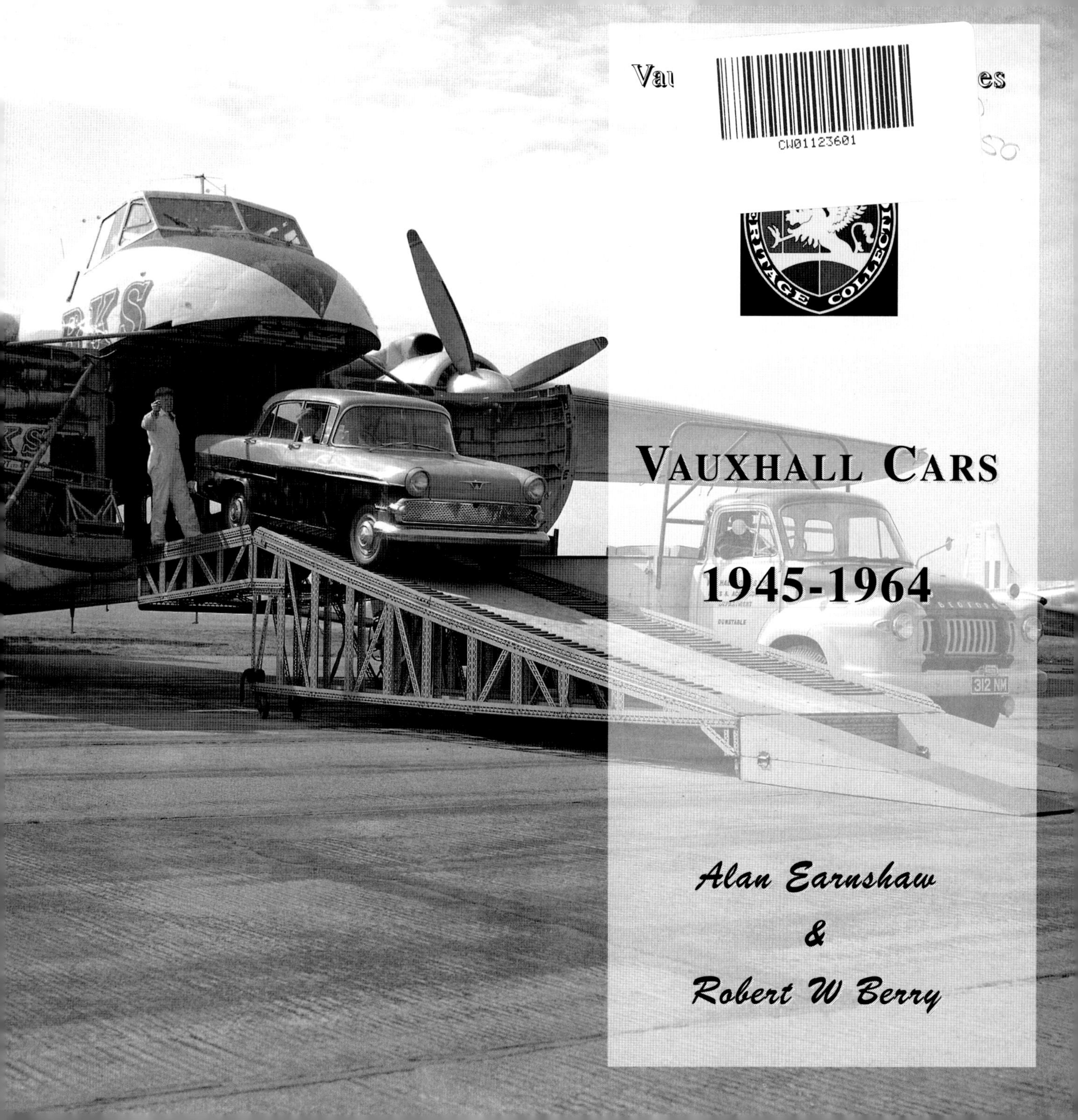

Vauxhall Cars
1945-1964

Alan Earnshaw

&

Robert W Berry

Contents

Introduction	3
From Marine Engines To Motor Cars	4
L-Type	6
E-Type	8
F-Type Victor	14
PA-Type 1957-1960	18
PA-Type 1960 - 1962	22
Colour Files	25
FB Victor & VX4/90	33
HA Viva	38
PB-Type	42
FC Victor 101 & VX4/90	48
PC Cresta	52

Front Cover: *This wonderful publicity photograph typifies the image of a carefree lifestyle that could be enjoyed by Vauxhall Victor owners, even in the basic FB saloon.*

Rear Cover Top: *In a Gypsy Red paint scheme this 1957 F-Type Victor Super, clearly shows the continuation of the famous 'Vauxhall Flutes' in the chrome trim on its wings.*

Rear Cover Bottom: *Again showing the chrome flutes, this preserved L-Type Velox, with its 6-cylinder engine is taken in period surroundings that are so evocative of motoring in the immediate post-war period.*

Title Page: *In this wonderful period view we see an early Series II F-type Victor disembarking from a BKS Bristol Freighter car transporter (powered by twin piston engines) probably at Lympe airport, whilst a Bedford TJ truck belonging to Vauxhall Motors stands alongside.*

This Page: *In at the start, the Vauxhall plant at Luton in 1905 with the latest cars lined up outside.*

ALL RIGHTS RESERVED

No Part of this publication may be reproduced, stored in a retrieval system, or transmitted, in any form or by any means, electronic, mechanical, photocopying, recording or otherwise, without prior permission in writing from the publishers.

ISBN 1-903016-44-4

Originally Published in 2000, as part of the
Nostalgia Road-Classic Marques Series as ISBN 1 903016 00 2

British Cataloguing in Publication Data
A catalogue record for this book is available from the British Library

---

The **Vauxhall Heritage Series**
is designed and published by
Trans-Pennine Publishing Ltd.
PO Box 10, Appleby-in-Westmorland
Cumbria, CA16 6FA
Tel. 017683 51053 - Fax. 017683 53558
e-mail trans.pennine@virgin.net
for

Vauxhall Heritage Services
Lynwood Heritage Services Ltd.
High Street, Princes End,
Titpton, West Midlands DY4 9HG
Tel. 0121 522 5566 - Fax: 0121 522 5565
World wide web: www.vauxhallheritage.com

Reprographics
Barnabus Design & Repro
Threemilestone, Truro
Cornwall, TR4 9AN
01872 241185

And Printed in Cumbria by
Kent Valley Colour Printers Ltd.
Shap Road Industrial Estate
Kendal, Cumbria LA9 6NZ
01539 741344

© Lynwood Heritage Services Ltd. & Trans-Pennine Publishin Ltd.,
© Text A. Earnshaw & R.W. Berry 2000 & 2001
© Photographs: Vauxhall Motors Ltd. (all rights reserved)

Foreword

I take great pleasure in writing the foreword for this book, which is part of a series on Vauxhall and Opel classic cars that I have commissioned to be published over the coming years. This book also marks the launch of **Vauxhall Heritage Services** whose mission is 'to provide parts, services and merchandise for the Vauxhall/Bedford/Opel classic car park on a worldwide basis.'

To achieve these objectives, Vauxhall Motors have entrusted the management and promotion of Vauxhall Heritage Services to my company, Lynwood Heritage Services Limited on a sole supplier basis. To complement this arrangement, I have struck a strategic partnership with Professor Alan Earnshaw and his team at Trans-Pennine Publishing Limited to publish and co-ordinate the research and writing of this series of books. This volume was first published in May 2000 as part of their Classic Marques series, but it has been subsequently revised and complemented with additional historic pictures that have recently come to light!

Above: *Some 50 years after the picture shown on the facing page was taken, the scene of things had dramatically changed at Luton and, with substantial investment in a modern plant, the company were ready to meet the challenges of the post-war era. Here we show a batch of E-Type cars coming off the production line in the 1950s with a Cresta leading, followed by a brace of Wyverns.*

At the time of the revision and re-publication of this book, we are also producing the next volume in the series, *Vauxhall Cars 1965-1984*. These two books will be followed by three more volumes, each of which will tell a 20-year part of Vauxhall's fascinating history. In the fullness of time, the five 56-page books will tell the centennial record of car production by the company - the last book being launched just before the 100th anniversary of the company is reached in 2003. I hope that you will take as much delight in reading these books, as we have had in preparing them.

Ron Atkins Tipton, June 2000

Above: *The tug* Westbourne *at Tilbury in 1891, fitted with a marine engine built by the Vauxhall & West Hydraulic Co.*

From Marine Engines To Motor Cars

It may well seem odd to commence this section with a picture of a Thames tug boat, and readers may well wonder if we have taken leave of our senses. Yet, what could be more appropriate to start a book on Vauxhall Cars than such a picture? It just so happens that Vauxhall, more commonly associated with Luton in Bedfordshire, owes its history to an estate on the south bank of the River Thames. This estate was granted to one Fulk le Breant, a mercenary knight who served the onerous King John. The name Fulks Hall became corrupted over the years, and the name Vauxhall took its place. Of course it still remains as a London suburb, but to motoring enthusiasts the world over, it is better known as a popular brand of motor vehicle that emerged from the famous works at Luton in Bedfordshire.

This series of books records a century of Vauxhall history each loosely spanning a 20 year story, in five publications. However, we begin some six centuries after Fulk le Breant, when a Scottish engineer by the name of Alexander Wilson established an Iron Works at Vauxhall, where he produced engines and pumps for the growing maritime industry. Located in Wandsworth Road, the company rapidly expanded but Wilson had left the company by 1894.

Times were changing and the steam engines for yachts, naval pinnaces and other small craft were rapidly being replaced by internal combustion engines. A demand for new, more powerful tugs in the latter part of the 19th-Century threatened Vauxhall's traditional business as the internal combustion engine developed, and began to supplant the smaller marine steam engines. Financial difficulties nearly brought about the end of Vauxhall in 1896, and a Mr J H Chambers was appointed as the Official Receiver. Nevertheless he turned the firm around and in 1897 it became known as the Vauxhall Ironworks Company Ltd. Before the year was out Chambers, and his Chief Engineer (F W Hodges) had designed and built a petrol engine for a new launch called the *Jabberwock*, and this engine (with refinements) probably became the basis for the first Vauxhall car in 1903.

A legacy of the Fulk le Breant estate that passed down to Vauxhall is seen in the firm's famous Griffin logo, which still forms the company logo at the start of the 21st-Century. This mythical beast, with its composite body of a lion and an eagle, was originally used on Fulk's coat of arms, but is better known to most people as the badge that has adorned thousands of Vauxhall cars.

The first of these cars was a 5hp model with a 989cc single-cylinder engine, and was to receive very favourable reviews when it first appeared. In the years that followed a range of progressive developments took place, and Vauxhall is still one of the major British car brands. This particular volume covers the firm's progress in the period from 1945 to 1964, which are the two most significant decades in the development of the modern motor car. The year 1945 saw the end of World War II, but it also saw Britain in a battered and bruised state after six years of total war. This war affected every sector of the British public, combatant and civilian alike, and it also dramatically changed the face of British motor manufacturing as well. During that war, the Vauxhall works became heavily involved in military vehicle and tank production, but car manufacture suffered as a result. In fact only 100 or so cars were produced at Luton during the war years, although 5,460 Churchill tanks and almost a quarter of a million trucks were built.

Immediately after the war, the Government demanded that export be given priority, and in the period up to October 1946, no less than 10,000 Bedford trucks were sent abroad. A few 10hp cars came out of the works in 1945, but it was not until 1946 that production properly resumed with H, I and J type cars. Thereafter Vauxhall went from strength to strength, raising the standard as they went. What is crucial about the two decades following 1945 is the way that Vauxhall set about capturing the growing market, producing popular cars with radical new styling and features that were often well ahead of their time.

As the private car-owner market expanded in the late-1950s and early-1960s, Vauxhall were poised to capture a major share. By 1959 they had built their two millionth car, and a new era dawned with the luxurious PA series with its modern trans-Atlantic styling. Yet for the average family man, upgrading from his motorcycle combination or bus travel, it was the advent of the little 1057cc HA Viva saloon in 1963 that made new car-ownership possible. More modern in styling than the Morris 1000, and more spacious than the BMC Mini, the Viva heralded a new approach as the era under consideration comes to a close. It was therefore an important 20-year period, and not one that anybody can dismiss lightly.

Top Right: *All the images in this book have been supplied by Vauxhall, but we make an exception to show this picture of a Vauxhall D-Type, in a two-tone grey livery, a 1937 saloon which is fairly representative of the kind of Vauxhall car in use in 1945. It is shown with Euan Jamieson on the Isle of Yell in the Shetlands in 1954. In the distance is the Isle of Unst, the most northerly part of the British Isles.* Gordon Jamieson

Bottom Right: *In reality we should have begun this section with a chapter on the 1946-1948 HIY and HIX models, but as these were really only postwar developments of pre-war models, they will be covered in the book Vauxhall Cars 1925-1944. For the moment we show a 1422cc HIX passing a Bedford OLAD dropside truck whilst in Cornwall on a 'photo-shoot' in 1946.*

THE L-TYPE 1948-1951

As will be appreciated from the previous chapter, car production at Luton had not been high during the war years and no real development had taken place. Accordingly when the hostilities ended, all Vauxhall had to offer was its pre-war production models, comprising of the H-, I- and J- types. Even then, most of what was produced was destined for export, and it was not until mid-1947 that things began to get easier. Around this time the government changed car taxation to a flat-rate from the previous horse-power related system. This spurred Vauxhall to up-rate its 10hp engine to 12hp, and adopted the I-Type power unit for its new L-Type models. The first of these cars was launched in 1948,

Ostensibly a new series, the L-Type's body shell was actually an updated H-Type with both a new front and a new rear end. The new front followed the standard practice of car design at that time, whereby the front wing flowed into the bonnet and (although a separate construction) still gave the impression of being an integral unit. The headlamps were now built into the front of the wings, and the rear-hinged bonnet swept down to a low radiator grill comprising of six horizontal chrome slats.

Above: *The Wyvern and the Velox had the same overall, and rather comfortable body style. It was usually painted black, but had a smattering of chrome on the badges, headlamp bezels, radiator grill, hub caps and along the famous Vauxhall bonnet flutes. Here we see two female models with a Velox, which had the period accessory of a two-band radio, but the dog shows little interest!*

The new rear end featured a protruding boot, and this gave considerably improved luggage accommodation over previous models. The boot also featured a self-supporting lid. The four doors of the L-Type, like its predecessor, were all hinged from the central pillar, thus making the two front doors front-opening.

Two models were offered, the four-cylinder Wyvern and the six-cylinder Velox. A column change three-speed gear box, with synchromesh on the two upper gears, was fitted to both cars. The 1442cc OHV Wyvern had a bore of 69.5mm and a stroke of 95mm and was fitted with a single Zenith carburettor. For the customer requiring better performance, the 2275cc Velox was the one to choose. It had the same bore as the Wyvern, but the stroke was slightly longer at 100mm - this gave the Velox a good 10mph more than the Wyvern's top speed of 60mph.

Externally, both models appeared identical but on the inside the Velox was far more lavishly appointed. It was provided with leather seats, as opposed to the Wyvern's cloth upholstery. However the Wyvern was later offered with leather seats as an optional extra at a cost of £20 (£375.50). The easiest way to tell the two cars apart was by the overriders fitted to the bumpers on the Velox. Another clue was the paint colour on the wheels and from a car-mad schoolboy's point of view, this was a dead giveaway; the Velox always had cream-painted wheels, whilst the Wyvern's were painted to match the body colour.

As mentioned the L-Type Wyvern and Velox shared the cabin of the H-Type, and this shows that the L-Type was really just a stop-gap model to satisfy the emerging postwar demand for new cars. Already a new series, the E-Type, was being developed but in the interim customers had to be satisfied. Even so, during its relatively short three-year production span, the L-Type had a few improvements. One notable change was the separate side-lights, which replaced the integral sidelight/headlamp arrangement of the earlier cars. The rear number plate was also moved from its original position just above the bumper and placed on the boot lid. A new Burman worm and peg steering box and king pins were fitted from 1949 onwards. Another change was in the new 'Metallic-Chrome' paintwork offered in blue, grey, green or fawn.

When introduced, the cars cost £447 (£8,392) for the Wyvern and £550 (£10,326) for the Velox. This actually made the Velox one of the World's cheapest six-cylinder saloon cars of the time. It was hardly a radical step forward into the brave new postwar world, but it did show indications of the new designs that were just around the corner. Already Vauxhall was gearing up for the 1950s, and they were soon 'Raising The Standard'. The dark days of the war years (which included a direct hit on the Luton plant by a German bomb that claimed 39 lives) were now firmly behind them and new and exciting Vauxhall models were just around the corner.

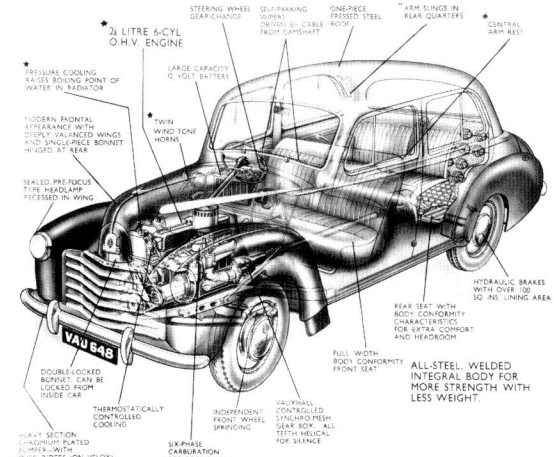

Top Right: *The two vehicles shown in this picture indicate the extensive and diverse range of products produced at the Luton plant in the late-1940s. On the left we see a Vauxhall L-Type saloon and on the right a Bedford OLAD truck (one of 13 variations of the O-Type commercial vehicles built between 1939 and 1953).*

Centre Right: *This fascinating 'cut-away' picture from a period publicity brochure shows the new 2.2 litre Vauxhall Velox L-Type. Although the reproduction is not quite as large as we would like to have used, it still clearly illustrates the vital components of the car and thus forms a unique illustration for this book. The registration plate on the car (VAU 648) gives away its identity as a Vauxhall six-cylinder 1948 saloon.*

Bottom Right: *In order to provide something new for 1948, Vauxhall took the 98-inch wheelbase HIY/HIX model, and gave it a completely re-styled front and back end. The 1203cc and 1442cc engine was up-rated to a 1442cc engine on the four-cylinder Wyvern, or a powerful 2275cc on the six-cylinder Velox illustrated here.*

Above: *'The Car You'll Enjoy Is A Vauxhall' was the company's main advertising slogan in the mid-1950s. This publicity picture of a 2.2 Cresta was used with the slogan, and its fine lines are shown off by the eye-catching two tone colour scheme.*

THE E-TYPE 1951-1957

Replacements for the dated L-Types were announced in August 1951, although the names Wyvern and Velox were retained for use on the new four- and six-cylinder models. The E-Type cars also initially retained the same power unit, but this was very much an interim measure as Vauxhall's new short stroke engines were in an advanced state of development.

In their body shape the E-Type Vauxhalls were completely new, and the design owed much to the Chevrolet Series G Styleline that General Motors was producing in America. Using a full width monocoque construction, the cars were to prove highly successful and 342,000 of them would be built before production finally came to an end in 1957.

Both the Wyvern and the Velox shared the same body style, which featured a straight-through wing line. A curved panoramic windscreen looked out over a wide bonnet, the lid of which was side-opening on the earlier models. A further feature of the bonnet was that it could be opened from either side or removed altogether for ease of access!

The E-Type's bonnet retained the famous flute on the side, whilst the Vauxhall badge was positioned on the leading edge. Below the bulbous nosed bonnet was a substantial radiator grill formed in a low, wide oval. This was divided by one horizontal bar that ran through the outer edges and ended below the headlamps, and one central vertical bar. The bumper was a relatively simple structure incorporating a slight recess. Once again the Velox had the luxury of over-riders.

The top of the front wings were set level with the base of the bonnet, but they protruded out over the wheels and the wheel arches swept down in a pleasing curve that ended at the leading edge of the front doors. The sides of the car featured a mock wing line on the rear wing (which looked rather like an inverted hockey stick). Chrome-finished, push-button door handles were set just below the through body line.

Top Right: *Taken on 30th January 1952, this picture shows the Luton assembly line, with workers putting together a number of E-Type Velox and Wyvern cars. The Cresta version would not be introduced until 1954.*

Bottom Right: *A study of Vauxhall's publicity photographs will reveal that many were taken in very exotic locations, thus conjuring the image that a Luton-made car could offer the glamour of foreign travel. The car seen beneath the Leaning Tower of Pisa is a Velox of 1954 vintage. Comments made in the text about the rear window lines are well illustrated in this picture, the smaller rear window itself was replaced in October 1955 by a larger rear screen, which was of a wrap-round curved design to offer a more panoramic view.*

The rear wings swept along to the tail lamps, which were contained in a chrome crescent-shaped housing situated at the top of a recess in the wings. The boot was another pleasing feature, and the sales brochures made much play about the easy loading it offered. The large, counter-balanced lid reached down almost to the rear bumper. The boot also had stowage for the spare wheel in a well below the boot floor. The rear window was much smaller than the front windscreen, and had a flat base but curved round to the roof line in a sweeping arc. Identification of the different models in the E-type series was much easier than it had been with its predecessor, as discreet chrome name plates were situated on the leading edge of the front wings. This feature, and a slightly more ornate bonnet badge on the Velox were the only real ways to quickly distinguish between the two models.

As stated, the early E-Type cars inherited their power units from their predecessors, but these developed a paltry 35bhp on the four-cylinder cars and 54bhp on the six-cylinder ones. This was clearly inadequate for the market at which Vauxhall were aiming their new models, but the problem had been clearly identified by the company and new engines were already in the design stage.

The new power units were launched in the Spring of 1952, and these had a bore diameter of 79.3mm and a stroke of 76.2mm. On the Wyvern this gave a capacity of 1508cc, and turned it in to what Vauxhall described as a 70mph car. The Velox was now good for 80mph, and could boast a 2262cc engine. Vauxhall favoured the 'Three on the Tree' transmission, as did Ford of Dagenham - was this a case of more Detroit influence one wonders?

Internally the car looked very handsome, and the most distinctive feature was the two-spoke steering wheel. This came in either a cream or a black finish, depending on the colour of the car's interior. The dashboard featured two circular instrument dials, one serving as a speedometer and mileage recorder, the other a temperature gauge and fuel gauge. The interior finish looked lavish, but a shortage of leather in the late 1940s had led the company to introduce a synthetic material called Vynide. The seats of both the Wyvern and the Velox used this material, as did the door panels on the Velox. The Velox interior also featured a two-tone colour scheme.

Top Left: *Not often shown in many transport books, but an integral part of any vehicle, are views of the engine compartment. This shows the early six-cylinder power unit fitted to the Velox, and the side-opening bonnet. Various improvements followed in the ensuing years, including a much more effective air filter.*

Centre Left: *This well-known photograph has appeared in several Vauxhall brochures over the years, but it is worth repeating once again as it shows a Velox competing in the Coronation Rally in Kenya. In the 1950s the eventing and competition side of Vauxhall began to assume considerable significance and whilst never as strong as it had been in the 'Hancock days' a few people in Vauxhall saw it as a very important means of promoting sales of standard cars.*

Bottom Left: *A view of the Luton assembly line on 29th November 1955, showing a number of E-Type cars; first of all we see a Velox, then a Wyvern and a Cresta. Identification can be easily made by the level of exterior chrome applied to the cars. It is interesting to note that many photographs show models going 'piece-meal' down the assembly rather than being sent in blocks of one particular model. Other pictures show that light commercial vehicles would also go down the line in and amongst the cars, thus adding to the variety on the shop floor.*

Various improvements were made to the cars during these early years, including a new facia panel in 1953. In June 1953 the bonnet saw a radical alteration, for Vauxhall changed from their side-opening arrangement to a more conventional rear-hinged bonnet. In October 1954 the 'most radical improvement to the range' came with the introduction of a top-line model, the Cresta, which was launched at the Earls Court Motor Show in October. The new model was a Deluxe version of the six-cylinder Velox, but could be instantly recognised by its two-tone paint scheme. The division between the colours being a thin chrome strip just below the windows.

In what the company called 'trans-Atlantic styling', the car was given white wall tyres and chrome hub caps (which featured the Griffin emblem in the centre). The Cresta logo was carried in script lettering on the lower left edge of the boot lid. A new bonnet and radiator grill was also introduced. The radiator grill was now a die-cast construction of short vertical bars, with chrome saucers at the outer ends to contain the side lamps/indicators. Above the grill ran a horizontal chrome bar, in which the Vauxhall name featured prominently.

The interior was completely revamped for the Cresta, and a new facia was provided. This had two large, recessed circular dials; one was directly in front of the driver with the speedometer, and one of an identical diameter in front of the passenger seat to take the radio speaker. Actually this was a clever piece of design planning, because the same dashboard could be used for either right-hand or left-hand drive models simply by swapping the speaker and instrument dials around. The added luxury of the Cresta warranted a two-tone (real) leather interior.

At the same time, the Wyvern and Velox models were also given a face-lift. They obtained the new facia panel, the new radiator and the new bonnet. The six-cylinder cars also obtained spats over the rear wheels. The new radiator grill did not last long, and in styling changes of October 1955, it was replaced by a chrome-plated pressing. This looked very similar to the previous design, but it was cheaper to produce and had fewer vertical bars. At this time all three models received deeper and wider front and rear windscreens. There were interior changes too, as a new roof lining material was applied. The two cheaper cars were given a new type of vinyl for their upholstery, but both six-cylinder models were given the luxury of arm-rest door pulls.

By 1956 the replacement models for the E-Type series were at an advanced stage of development, but it would be the following year before they were introduced. In the interim Vauxhall made yet further improvements to the E-Type models in time for the Earls Court Motor Show. Engines on these improved models benefited by the fitting of a new Zenith carburettor, whilst another improvement was the introduction of electric windscreen wipers. The 1957 cars had yet another new style radiator grill, this time one of fine horizontal bars. New tail lamps and a thin chrome waist band, were new features. This band had a slight dip on the rear doors, but then rose again to follow the rear wing line. On the Cresta a second chrome band was situated above the first, and the area between was painted a contrasting shade to the body colour. One further development in 1957 was the involvement of external coachbuilders who, with the permission of Vauxhall, produced an estate car version of the Velox. The two firms involved were Martin Walter Ltd. of Cheriton Road, Folkestone and The Grosvenor Carriage Company Ltd. of Kimberley Road London.

Top Right: *A 1955 four-cylinder Wyvern pictured in a sylvan rural location again features in this publicity picture. Closer examination will reveal that parts of the radiator grill are finished in body colour paint, it will also be noted that the car does not feature spats around the wheel arches, although they had been applied to the six-cylinder model by this time.*

Centre Right: *In this view, we can see the spats applied to the wheels on a six-cylinder Cresta. Note how the side trim gives a suggestion of motion, and the publicity photograph taken on an aerodrome conveys an air of freedom. For those interested, the airliner is a 55-seat Boeing 377 Stratocruiser (designed in 1947) and here employed in the service of the British Overseas Aircraft Corporation.*

Bottom Right: *Variations on horse-power, in yet another typical publicity shot taken at a stable (the Vauxhall photographer must have liked horses as well as aircraft)! Here a young rider admires a 1956 Cresta, which may well have been painted in the popular maroon and silver straw colour scheme. The white wall tyres, chrome trim, and powerfully styled front end give a distinct 1950s trans-Atlantic look, and the American styling influences from the Chevrolet (although subtly toned down for the UK market) are clearly obvious.*

The Grosvenor Estate had a noticeable V-shaped pillar behind the rear passenger door and a split tailgate. On this 5th door the upper half was spring-loaded and released by a press-button situated in a wide handle. The lower half of the door was released by an interior handle. The rear seat could be converted into a double bed, and like the front seats it was covered in a soft durable material in a checked pattern. Alternatively the rear seat could be folded away (long before the days of Flex-7 technology), leaving a large load space area finished in dark-faced plywood protected by wearing strips in polished aluminium.

Grosvenor offered their conversion painted in a choice of monotone colours or two-tone colours. The two-tone colours were as follows, Desert Yellow with Mistral Grey, Mistral Grey/Moon Grey, Moon Grey/Mistral Grey, Bamboo Green/Mistral Grey, Mistral Grey/Apache Brown, Apache Brown/Canyon Red and Apache Brown/Desert Yellow. The monotone colours were Mistral Grey, Canyon Red, Apache Brown, Bamboo Green, Desert Yellow, Moon Grey and Ebony Black.

Some Grosvenor-bodied estates were, however, found in other colours, because in addition to modifying production line saloons, the firm would also convert existing or second-hand cars. The cost of this service was £230 (£3,680), and whilst it was a substantial figure at the time, the *Farmer's Guardian* stated that this was 'a reasonably affordable way to achieve all-round versatility, with a reliable vehicle offering a spacious goods compartment and two roomy passenger seats. At the weekend it converts back to a five seat family saloon, with a reasonable compartment for the dogs, guns, etc.'

Top & Centre Left: *Although the E-Type had become very popular as saloon cars, there was still a large gap in the range offered as production models. Ford had the same situation with the cars it made at Dagenham, but they had successfully got round the problem by working with outside body-builders who could convert saloon cars to estate or convertible models. Vauxhall's main association was with the Folkestone firm of Martin Walter, and here we see two views that show the conversion that this company offered to existing Vauxhall owners. On an existing car, such as this Velox, the two-tone paint scheme split at the waist, as opposed to the sandwich effect on the new car conversions which started using cars off the production line in 1957.*

Bottom Left: *Another firm offering conversions from the standard saloon was Grosvenor. This three-quarter rear view of a Velox estate shows to good effect the split tailgate and the curious 'v-shaped' pillar.*

Bottom Right: *Martin Walter's new Dormobile estate car converted a production line saloon into a vehicle that offered a load carrying space, a shooting brake or even a vehicle in which one could go 'camping'. Several Vauxhall pictures actually show an attractive female model laying recumbent in a sleeping bag or under a travel rug in the back of one of these estate conversions. (Sorry chaps the wife wouldn't let me put them in the book) So, you'll have to be content with this rather bland 'showroom' picture without a model. Note the Bedford CA pick-up truck conversion also by Martin Walter.*

Martin Walter's well-known Dormobile (dormitory mobile) development on the Bedford chassis began here, as the estate version of the E-Type featured a folding front seat. This gave a sleeping area of 6ft 9in x 3ft 5in, not a lot of room but it offered 'the freedom to roam' (probably in more ways than one)! Externally the Martin Walter Dormobile had a one-piece tailgate made from plastic. When opened this top-hinged tailgate provided support and anchorage for the 'tent' that came with the car. When this tent was packed away, it could be stowed neatly with its alloy poles inside a cylindrical container that was provided. The rear suspension was given 'stiffer' springing, resulting in a much firmer ride than the saloon. The overall weight, at 22½-cwt, was actually slightly less than the saloon. The Dormobile cost £741 plus purchase tax of half as much again, making a price of £1,112.17.0d (£17,250) for the new estate.

The other interesting versions on the E-Type were built at the General Motors Holden plant in Australia. Besides building the conventional saloon, Holden also built several other models. These included a handsome two-door convertible known as the Vagabond, a Woody Estate and a 10-cwt pick-up/utility truck known as the Coupe-Utility, but better known in the outback as the Ute.

The Wyvern model of the E-Type was discontinued in January 1957, at a time when Vauxhall changed their policy and decided that rather than continue fitting four-cylinder and six-cylinder engines in the same body shell, they would produce two different body types. The Wyvern was therefore to be superseded by a completely new design, which was to be known as the Vauxhall Victor when introduced in March 1957. The two six-cylinder cars were destined to have a slightly longer life, and they remained in production until September 1957. At this time they too were replaced by a completely new design, but once again both six-cylinder models shared the same body shell. These were the PA Vauxhall Velox and Cresta, which were launched to an appreciative public in October 1957.

In all some 5,313 Wyverns were produced with the long-stroke engine during 1951-2, and a further 105,275 were built with the new engine between 1952 and 1957. As for the Velox, some 13,277 long-stroke engine models, and 222,019 cars with the 2,262cc engine were produced in the corresponding period. The Cresta was only ever built with the newer design of engine, but in its production life some 166,504 were built in the period from 1954 to 1957. In all a staggering total of over half a million E-Type Vauxhalls.

F-TYPE VICTOR 1957-1961

Just as the E-Type series Wyvern, Velox and Cresta owed much of their styling to the 1949 Chevrolet sedans, one can also see an American influence in the new F-Type Vauxhall Victor. The F-Type can be firmly linked with the 1955 Chevrolet, but it is curious that Vauxhall decided to develop a wider share of the market by using a more compact body shell on the new four-cylinder saloon. Introduced to the motoring public in March 1957, the new Victor broke fresh ground by featuring trans-Atlantic styling featuring a wrap-round windscreen both front and rear. To allow this the door pillars were stepped back and this gave a fully panoramic outlook for the occupants.

The famous Vauxhall flutes were now 'javelin-like' on the sides of the front wing. They then tapered back along the front doors to end at a 'vanishing point' on the rear side doors. Another horizontal line ran from the base of a curiously scallop-shaped pressing in the rear doors. These features, along with the rake of the front and rear screens, and the sweep of the front wheel arch (the rear one was lower) all gave the impression of motion, a feature that can be determined even from the static picture shown above.

Above: *To capture the spirit of the Victor name, publicity pictures were taken at RAF Wytan in March 1957, alongside what was then Britain's most modern 'nuclear deterrent aircraft'. This aircraft, was the stylish Handley Page Victor. It was fitted with four Bristol Siddley Sapphire 202 turbojets, and was actually the third of the RAF's new V-bombers. The prototype first flew in December 1952, but it took until February 1956 for the first production aircraft to take to the air. Even then their service life was marred by a series of engine problems until the original power units were replaced with the more powerful Rolls-Royce Conway engines.*

As seen from the picture above, the bonnet had two pronounced 'ribs', which swept down to a low, wide radiator grill that featured a honeycomb pattern. At the outer ends of this grill were situated the side lamp/indicator lights, which were set at the same slight camber as the outer ends of the radiator grill. This gave a harmonious, and stylish front end appearance. Beneath this the otherwise plain bumper featured two 'bullet-like' projections on the outer ends. At the rear end, the tail-lights were incorporated in vertical units set into the rather high wings. The wings themselves were level with the base of the rear screen, making for confident manoeuvring in reverse gear.

The actual vehicles were of unitary construction, with two longitudinal box-section members in the underbody. This provided the mounting points for the rear spring shackles and a detachable front cross member. In turn this cross member carried the front suspension assemblies and the front engine mounting. The rear engine mounting was carried on a cross-member that passed beneath the clutch housing, and was bolted to the box section body members. A transverse pressing acted as the cabin floor, and provided a mounting frame for the front seats. A second pressing gave anchorage points for the front end of the semi-elliptic rear springs (the front suspension being independent coil springs and wishbones). Further strengthening of the body was provided by a cruciform pressing between the rear wheel arches, and this both held up the rear parcel shelf and also provided support for the back of the rear seat.

Although powered by a straight four-cylinder engine, which was based on the former Wyvern power unit, the Victor's engine had a number of significant improvements, including an entirely new cylinder head. Bore and stroke were 99.37mm x 76.2mm, and this gave a displacement of 1507cc. A Zenith VN34 carburettor replaced the 30VIGH unit that had been fitted on the Wyvern.

During February 1958, Vauxhall announced the introduction of the Vauxhall Victor estate car, a unique step forward as this was the company's first 'in-house production' estate. It was to feature a one-piece tailgate and a new one-piece roof panel. Where the roof panel covered the load-space area, the pressing was slightly depressed and incorporated strengthening ribs. The luggage area was now a very spacious 22 cubic feet, or 45 cubic feet if the rear seats were folded down. This was a significant improvement over the 10.5 cubic feet in the boot of the conventional saloon. Also in 1958 Vauxhall offered the option to have the Victor with 'Newton Drive' two pedal automatic transmission. This was available throughout the range of four-cylinder cars at the extra cost of £25.10s.0d including purchase tax. At about £300 in today's currency that was quite a bargain, when one considers the £950 cost of an automatic gearbox on a 1.6 litre Vectra or Astra at the time of writing. Whilst talking about prices we might mention that the prices of the Victor range were as follows; Basic Saloon £748.7s.0d (£8,979.60), Super Saloon £781.7s.0d (£9,375.60) and Estate £931.7s.0d (£11,175.6).

Five different paint colours were offered for the basic Victor, namely, Charcoal Grey, Empress Blue, Laurel Green, Shantung Beige, or black. The Super was produced in any of these colours, but there was also the option to have Harvest Yellow, Horizon Blue or Gypsy Red. The estate cars often supported a roof panel painted in a contrasting colour to the body shade.

After almost two years of production, the F-Type Victor was revamped. Although it was identical with the earlier version in many ways, the Series II had a smoother, cleaner shape. The scallop shape in the rear door panels had vanished, and the chrome side flutes were extended into a fine chrome band running the full length of the body to give the car a longer look.

Above: *This British School of Motoring Vauxhall Victor Series 1 F-Type, is pictured in a period when many housewives were taking to the road - and although their husbands trusted them with most things, the family car was not one of them. A boom in motoring schools ensued! Another of the companies who put the Victor to this use was the Enfield School of Motoring who operated a large fleet of these cars in the late-1950s.*

Below: *As this June 1958 picture shows, the 100,000th Victor rolled off the Luton production line just 15 months after the launch of the car. This averaged the staggering total of 1,538 cars every week during that time.*

Top Left: *We now have a trio of pictures showing Series II Victors, the first of which is taken on the M1 motorway near to its junction with the A6. In the front row we see a PADY Cresta, a Victor Series II Super Estate, and Series II saloon. The picture was taken just prior to the 1959 Motor Show, and it is safe to state that it would be virtually impossible to recreate such a publicity photo shoot today!*

Centre Left: *Although it was like taking coals to Newcastle, Pontiac Motors distributed the F-Type Victor and the PA Cresta for General Motors in the USA. This Series II had its roof painted tartan, presumably for a special customer - an expatriate Scots perhaps?*

Bottom Left: *Returning to the theme of great days out and happy holidays, this Vauxhall publicity picture (reputedly taken in Norfolk) shows an F Type Victor Super. The car clearly shows the continuing American influence, and this time its genesis can be traced to the 1955 Chevrolet. Of course it was very much 'anglicised', but nevertheless its parentage can still be traced.*

On the Series II cars, the radiator grill was extended into a full-width unit with integral sidelight clusters. The lower front and rear wings lost their outward bulge, and a new, sleeker, wrap-round bumper was fitted. Just one central rib was seen in the bonnet pressing, and the front end also had a brand new bonnet badge. Internally new box-pleated upholstery was used on improved seats, and the same fabric also made matching door panels.

A new model was added to the range at the same time, in which refinements included individual front seats upholstered in two-tone leather. The seats themselves were adjustable for height and rake to complement the standard sliding gear. This new model was the Vauxhall Victor Deluxe, and its promotional sales material hinted it was 'THE CAR' for the well-to-do middle class family.

During August 1960 even more refinements were made to the Series II range. One of the most obvious changes was the radiator grill, which now consisted of five horizontal bands. The Vauxhall name was also spelt out in letters along the leading edge of the bonnet in place of the badge that had been used previously. The model's name was also shown in a chrome badge carried on the leading part of the flutes running along the car side. The headlamp hoods were also given new bright-work, by means of a fine chrome band. At the other end of the car, the most obvious change was the rear windscreen, which was now much deeper than before. Inside a new, re-designed facia panel and other improvements continued to ensure the car's popularity with the public.

The basic Victor was still available in a choice of five colours, but these were now black, Forge Blue, Silver Grey, Regency Cream, or Versailles Green. A further three colours, maroon, Havana Brown, and Royal Blue were available on the Super. The Deluxe models were available in seven colours, basically those on the Super, with the exception of the Regency Cream. Mind you, you could have the Deluxe in two-tone colours at no extra cost.

Also available as a two-tone car, the estate models were supplied in Silver Grey/black, Versailles Green/Silver Grey, Forge Blue/Silver Grey, or Regency Cream/Forge Blue. The De-luxe was available in a choice of six colours, this time Silver Grey/black, Royal Blue/Forge Blue, Versailles Green/black, maroon/Silver Grey, and Havana Brown/Regency Cream.

The F-Type Victor was an exceptionally popular model and by the time it was superseded by the FB Vauxhall Victor in September 1961, a total production figure of 390,745 had been achieved. It is also important to record three of the important events that occurred at the Luton works during its production life. Firstly the work force had risen to 22,000 as opposed to the 13,000 employees in 1953. Secondly, a capital investment programme of £36 million (£576,000,000) that had commenced in 1954 had helped the company to reach an annual production figure of around 100,000 cars a year. Thirdly, as a result of the first two factors, the annual company turnover had reached a staggering £76 million (in other words £912,000,000 in today's money) by the end of the 1950s. In 1959 the Luton plant turned out its two millionth car, itself quite a milestone, but an exceptionally important fact to note is that the plant had taken from 1905 to 1954 to make the first million cars. It made the next million inside just five years!

Top Right: *The Vauxhall Envoy may well be a car that many readers have never heard about, and probably for good reason as this was a car made specifically for the North American market. It was based on the F-Type Victor, but there were significant differences. The side trim, radiator grill, side lights, and larger tail light clusters are all obvious features. Another variation was the Sherwood Estate, which was marketed in both Canada and the United States as a small compact family car and targeted especially at affluent families as 'the second car' for the school run or shopping trips.*

Centre Right: *This is the British estate car version in the F Type Victor series, this time based on the Super model in the second series. Again using a female model with seven pieces of luggage, the picture is designed to show how spacious the Victor's load compartment was. With the rear seats folded down, the load space (whilst not quite to the standard of my modern Zafira) is still very spacious. The rubbing strips on the floor are also clearly evident, as is the self-supporting counter-balanced tailgate, no signs of gas struts here! Sadly only a few of the Victor estate cars have survived into preservation.*

Bottom Right: *This late Series II Victor Deluxe, shows the new style radiator grill made up of fine horizontal chrome-plated bands. It has also been given a much larger rear windscreen, offering considerably better visibility. The bumpers were now of a much more conventional design than those on the earlier model, and inside a redesigned facia had been installed. In all almost a third of a million F-Types were produced, and this sales figure was undoubtedly assisted by their 'American' look which is shown to good effect in this illustration.*

17

PA SERIES 1957-1960

The history of these cars neatly divides into two halves, and it also links neatly with the factory expansion we discussed in the last section. This expansion and improvement finally made it possible for Vauxhall to change from using just one single bodyshell for all the models it produced, and thus enabled the firm to produce different models for different markets. We have already described the changes for the four-cylinder car, but the six-cylinder E-Type cars remained in production after the introduction of the F-Type Victor. This led the motoring press to speculate that 'something new was in the air', and it certainly was. All was to be revealed at the 1957 Paris Motor Show, when Vauxhall unveiled their beautiful, sleek and very, very stylish six-seat saloon. It was not only radical in its body style, but the car was also completely new both bodily and mechanically.

Although being five inches longer, two inches wider and four and a half inches lower than the E-Type Velox and Cresta, a certain family likeness was retained. Styling features included a substantial Triplex wrap-round front windscreen, which harmonised at the back with a three-piece rear screen that employed thin pillars that had a pressed spine incorporated into them. At the front end the really wide bonnet had its outer sides rising to the centre line of the wing, whilst the front edge curved down to the low, wide radiator grill. Below this came the bumper, the outer sections of which curved round the corners of the front wings.

The leading edge of the bonnet had the Vauxhall name spelled out in individual chrome letters, whilst chrome strips finished off the bonnet lip and formed a slight hood above the headlamps. A continuing line of chrome trim ran along the sides of the car, ending at a point on the rear wings just before the tall oval tail light units.

Top Left: *Seen at the 43rd International Motor Show on 22nd October 1957 is the Vauxhall range of cars for 1958. From left to right we have four F Type Victors, two PA Crestas and two PA Velox.*

Top Right: *As the banner proclaims, this is the '1st of the 1958 Vauxhall Sixes', coming off the production line on 10th October 1957. Wheel discs, lack of bonnet badge, and white wall tyres suggest that this is a 2.2 PAS Velox.*

Bottom Right: *In addition to the UK sales, the PA Velox and Cresta found an immediate export market, with many cars going to Australia, South Africa and the Middle East in particular. Lack of badge, wheel trims etc. on what seems to be an export Velox makes identification problematic, but these items were usually stored inside the vehicle during transit.*

A low flite started at the rear door handle and, growing progressively, it carried along the top of the rear wing to terminate in the rear indicator unit. On the nearside, just below the rear windscreen pillar, the fuel filler cap was located and this gave access to the 10.8 gallon capacity tank. Between the rear wings a wide, spacious boot (with dedicated stowage for the spare wheel and tool kit) was provided. The self-supporting boot lid also carried the number plate, which was located before it dropped down to meet the body just above the bumper.

Both the cheaper Velox and the more refined Cresta shared identical mechanical specifications, and their new six-cylinder engine was a development of the four-cylinder unit in the new F-Type Victor. (The same over head valve 2262cc engine was also fitted into the last of the E-Type Velox and Cresta cars). Fitted with the new Zenith 34VNT down-draught carburettor it had a 79.4mm x 76.2mm bore and stroke. Transmission was via a 3-speed gearbox, with synchromesh on all forward gears, and controlled by a column-mounted gear lever. A Borg & Beck 8-inch dry-plate clutch and a Hardy-Spicer propeller shaft transferred power to the hypoid bevel final drive.

In the cabin the Velox used Vynide for the upholstery and Novon for the door panels, both materials being supplied by the Leathercloth Industries division of ICI. The Cresta buyer had a choice of leather, Elastofab, or nylon and Elastofab. Standard equipment on the Velox included arm-rests on all four doors, a folding armrest on the rear seat, dual tone horns, front courtesy lights operated by the doors, child-locks, interior roof lamp and speed wiper. The Cresta had all these, but it was also given a heater/defroster, screen washer, courtesy lights on all four doors, cigarette lighter, an electric clock, and a stainless steel moulding to the side windows. The Cresta also boasted a bonnet emblem, full diameter wheel discs and white wall tyres.

The Velox was offered in eight single tone colours; black, Dover White, Farina Grey, Laurel Green, Mountain Rose, Empress Blue, Gipsy Red and Wedgewood Blue. The same shades were available for the Cresta, plus five two-tone schemes Laurel Green/Dover White, Farina Grey/Charcoal Grey, Empress Blue/Wedgewood Blue, Mountain Rose/Charcoal Grey, or black/Dover White.

During 1958 one or two improvements were introduced for the 1959 models, noticeably a revision in paint colours which saw the following shades introduced: Royal Glow, Imperial Ivory, Laurel Green, Royal Blue, Haven Blue, Charcoal Grey, Silver Grey and black. The two-tone schemes were Royal Glow, Royal Blue, Charcoal Grey, Silver Grey or black, with Imperial Ivory as the second colour applied to the roof, boot deck and back end. In May 1959 Friary Motors of Basingstoke offered an estate car conversion to the PA Vauxhalls, and gave back seat passengers an extra 1½ inches of headroom. The load space behind was generous, but when the rear seats were not in use it extended to a generous 71in x 40in. Access to the load space area was by means of a one-piece, top-hinged tailgate. The spare wheel and tool kit were located beneath the platform floor, but the fuel filler had to be relocated down to the nearside rear wing. Five leaf springs were fitted, as opposed to the four springs on the saloon, and six-ply tyres also came as standard. Eight two-tone colour schemes were offered, or it also came in black. However, few of the Friary estates were built on the early PA models, as the series was completely revived in September 1959.

The 1959 prices were Velox saloon £929 (£11,148), Velox Friary Estate £1,222.5s (£14,667), Cresta saloon £1,014 (£12,168) and the Cresta Friary Estate at £1,308 (£15,696). These early models are designated PAD for the Cresta and PAS for the Velox. Several of them have been preserved and they are often mistaken, by a modern generation, as being 'old American cars'. One shudders! One lovely survivor is PAD 22504 (HGL 574), which was bought by a good friend of ours, Colin Moorhouse, back in 1986.

Top Left: *Pictured here at the 1958 Motor Show, the Vauxhall stand features a pair of Crestas finished in two-tone colour scheme (roofs in Dover White), along with two early Victors. Note how the sleek style of the Vauxhalls seem to date their contemporaries on other stands.*

Centre Left: *The prototype PA Velox estate car built by Friary Motors of Basingstoke, appeared extensively in both Vauxhall and Friary publicity material. The badge seen above the rear door pillar was only used on the prototype, and on production models the F Type Victor badge was used.*

Bottom Left: *Clearly showing the three-piece window arrangement employed on the early Vauxhall PAs. This style, unique in Britain, was however employed in America on other General Motors cars such as the Oldsmobile. Another 'American' feature is seen in the rear wings, with their fin-shape incorporating the indicators in the upper tip as can be clearly identified in this view. With plain wheel hubs and no bright trim around the windows, the car shown here is obviously the PA Velox. The broad side trim, running the length of the car, identifies this as an earlier model, as later PAs had a slightly narrower section and also a one-piece rear window!*

Right: *In all its glory, the Vauxhall stand at the 1958 Scottish Motor Show reveals a PAD Cresta sitting centre stage.*

PA SERIES 1960-1962

By September 1959 the PA series, whilst mechanically still the same, had received a cosmetic face-lift. The split three-piece rear windscreen was gone, and replaced by a single wrap-round screen. The ribs in the roof had also gone, whilst a new radiator grill (with a gently curved top) was fitted. The chrome side strips were also replaced, this time by a narrower strip at the same height which ran down the full length of the car. Thereafter the strip would serve as the dividing point for the two-tone colour models, the roof and panels below the strip being one colour, with a second colour sandwiched between. The single tone colours for the Velox and the Cresta were maroon, Regency Cream, Royal Blue, Banff Blue. Silver Grey, Kewanee Green, Coronade Yellow or black.

Above: *You may well have heard of the 'Royal Estate', well here it is! This PADX Cresta with a Friary Estate conversion (MYT 1) was supplied to Her Majesty Queen Elizabeth.*

On the Cresta there were five two-tone schemes, maroon and Kewanee Green, Royal Blue and black (all with Silver Grey) or Coronade Yellow and Regency Cream. Vynide was used for upholstery on the Velox, in a choice of four colours (maroon, grey, brown or blue) depending on the body shade. The Cresta could be upholstered in leather or Nylon and Elastofab.

To distinguish between the new cars and the earlier models, the chassis plates on the newer models were PADY for the Cresta and PASY on the Velox. These models were however only produced for around one year, as a new engine was then introduced to power the 6-cylinder Vauxhalls.

Top Left: *Apparently showing its proud new owners touring central London, this PADX Cresta circumnavigates Piccadilly Circus in a maroon/grey livery. This was of course another publicity shot, which may be given away by its Luton registration plate 67 CBM - this number plate also appears in another publicity picture, this time on a Bedford CA van.*

Centre Left: *This rear-three-quarter view of the PADX Cresta shows to good effect the changes from the earlier model Crestas. Comparing this view with that on page 20 will demonstrate the new one-piece rear window and the tail-light clusters that now incorporate the indicators.*

Bottom Left: *The 113bhp 2.6-litre PADX Vauxhall Cresta was aimed at a very stylish, class conscious market, which was coming very pronounced in the late-1950s. The fact that many of the pictures in the archive show people in quite 'well-to-do' or prosperous clothing, clearly indicates the type of customer that Vauxhall were seeking to attract.*

A significant factor in Vauxhall's increasing sales at this time was the reduction in Purchase Tax, and as far as the improved PA cars were concerned this gave prices of £929.0s.10d (£11,148) for the Velox and £1,014.0s.10d (£12,168) on the Cresta in 1959. The following year saw the arrival of the new engine and yet another face-lift, on models now designated PASX (Velox) and PADX (Cresta). The engine was now 2651cc, developing a maximum 113bhp, a substantial increase of 31bhp over the previous power unit.

The face-lift saw the incorporation of new sidelight units at the front, whilst new tail lights incorporated the rear indicators. A new thin chrome band now ran from the apex of the wrap-round windscreen, passing down the window pillars and running below the door windows before terminating at the end of the rear wing flites. Once again this band would be used as the dividing line for the two-tone colour schemes. The upholstery on the Velox was also improved, and in addition to the Vynide a woven Tygan Rayon material was available. An optional extra for the new 6-cylinder cars was the Laycock-de-Normanville overdrive unit, which cost £63.15s (£765). This was controlled by a switch fitted to the dashboard, and operated on the second and third gears in the 3-speed box.

By October 1960 Luton were turning out an automatic gearbox called Hydra-matic, which had been developed by General Motors for their new compact cars in the USA. A fluid-coupling type of transmission provided three forward ratios and reverse, and the six-position selection lever was mounted on the steering column. The extra cost for this option was a mere £170 (£2,040). One novel feature I recall from my uncle's Cresta, was the horizontal speed indicator, which had a scale reading that changed from green to amber at 30mph and from amber to red at 60mph.

New colour schemes were once again adopted, this time the choice being black, Royal Blue, Forge Blue, Silver Grey, Versailles Green, maroon, Regency Cream, Havana Brown and Lime Yellow. Seven two-tone schemes were available on the Cresta, using the same 'sandwich idea', but with the roof colour also being applied to the outer sides of the flites.

To quote the colour options again would be getting a bit monotonous, but if anyone wants to know, please feel free to write in and ask us. The problem of keeping track of colours is even more pronounced, because in 1961 they were changed again, when the Velox could be bought in 14 different hues, whilst the Cresta had 15 monotones and nine duo-tone schemes.

At the time the second colour changes were made to the range in 1961, there were also a number of cosmetic changes as well, but the design was seen as 'dated' and (with the new FB Victor already on the market), 1962 would see the introduction of the new PB series. Nevertheless, in the interim the PA did receive some improvements, notably front disc brakes, which aided performance considerably. The car was also given 14-inch wiper blades and the option of single front seats. The Velox also had the luxury of fitted floor carpets front and rear, whilst the Cresta got Rayon carpeting and a wood-grain effect finish to the facia panel. Friary still provided the official estate car conversions until the PA was superseded by the PB in 1962, but after this change the conversions would be carried out by Martin Walter.

Top Left: *A selection of PA Cresta estate car pictures. This PASY Velox, seen in Hampshire's Loddon Valley not far from the Friary factory, is pictured wearing the alternative two-tone colour scheme that divided at the waist line. The Cresta paint scheme was a sandwich effect, and white-wall tyres were standard, but came as an extra on the Velox.*

Centre Left: *The next image is an excellent view of a PADX Cresta with the Friary estate conversion. This vehicle is probably in the Havana Brown and Regency Cream colour scheme, and clearly shows the repositioned fuel filler cap on the estate car. Also of note are the new design of tail lights, the new style bumper and the later style of Friary badge, which is again located on the top of the rear door pillar.*

Bottom Left: *In a two-tone livery of Dusk Rose and Lilac Haze, this PADX Cresta carries yet another Friary estate car conversion and is pictured in London's Covent Garden produce market. Like many of Vauxhall's publicity pictures, this view captures the atmosphere of the early-1960s, in what is obviously a real Victorian setting. Amidst the architecture and atmosphere, the Cresta is seen in the company of a plethora of British Road Service lorries, with a private operator AEC Mammoth Major to the fore. All that is needed to complete this scene, is that other well-known Covent Garden character, Eliza Doolittle from 'My Fair Lady'!*

Above: *This E-Type Wyvern, was the four-cylinder successor to the L-Type Wyvern, which went out of production in 1951. It initially had the 1442cc engine of its predecessor, but in 1952 it was given the new short-stroke 1507cc power unit. This particular model is unusual in the fact that it carries wheel spats, over-riders and white wall tyres which were normally only fitted on the six-cylinder Velox. As can be recognised from the setting, this is a recent picture of one of the preserved cars in the Vauxhall Heritage collection.*

Right: *In this period picture dating from around 1949, we see the L-Type model produced between 1948 and 1951. This particular car is the four-cylinder Wyvern, as can be identified by the body-coloured wheels and the lack of over-riders on the bumper. Note the chrome trim on the bonnet flutes and the front opening front (rear-hinged) doors which were better known as 'suicide doors' due to the fact that they could come open whilst the car was in motion.*

Above: *A late-1956 view showing the last of the E-Types, and the last series in which Luton used just one body style for its different models. In March 1957 the Wyvern would be replaced by the F-Type Victor, and seven months later the PA Velox and Cresta models would replace the six-cylinder E Types. The car shown above is an E Type Cresta, as distinguished by the contrasting body flash and white wall tyres. It was introduced in October 1956 for the 1957 market. Note the de-misting panel fitted on the rear windscreen.*

Left: *Again carrying white wall tyres, and posed on the north coast of Cornwall in the mid-1950s, this is an E-Type Cresta. With the model code EIPC, this six-cylinder saloon had a short-stroke 2262cc engine. The fact that this is the later model E-Type Cresta, can be determined by the larger rear windscreen and the lower styling line dividing the two-tone paint work: the earlier models had the dividing line just below the window.*

Above: *Following the introduction of the F-Type in 1957, Vauxhall introduced new styling changes early in 1959. These changes are shown in this Vauxhall Victor, 6549 AH, which is also part of the Vauxhall Heritage collection based at Luton. Compare the bonnet, radiator grill, bumpers and rear doors of this car with the original 1957 F-Type shown elsewhere in the book. This is an early Series two Victor, as noted by the fact that the later models had a larger rear windscreen and different radiator grill.*

Right: *This Series II F-Type Victor and I have a particular infinity, as I had the privilege of driving this car from the Vauxhall Heritage Centre around the Goodwood Motor Racing Circuit in September 2000 during the Heritage Revival Weekend. Together we had some notable passengers during the weekend, including the famous racing driver Stirling Moss, but I'm sure that his driving round the circuit was far more proficient than mine!*

Above: *So typical of the publicity pictures taken at the time, these 'posed' views show two of the very first PA models introduced in October 1957. Mountain Rose was the description given to this delicate shade of pink shown in the upper view, and the white wall tyres were another distinctive feature. The period evening clothes are another remarkable feature of this picture, and they clearly show the type of market that Vauxhall aimed this stylish model at.*

Left: *Whenever I attend motor shows or rallies with the Vauxhall Heritage Photograph Display, I can guarantee that the one range of Vauxhall cars that attracts the most attention is the PA series. It is quite incredible how many people come up and reveal their fond memories of the model; this is hardly surprising for this was a car so far ahead of its contemporaries, that it created a lasting impression on many people's minds. Little wonder when Vauxhall used pictures like this to promote its image for the late-1950s.*

Above: *When the F-Type Victors were withdrawn in 1961, their trans-Atlantic styling vanished and the replacement looked very bland. Yet the FB-Victors were actually sheep in wolves clothing, and their 1508cc engines developed 55bhp. The wheelbase and track length were increased over the F-Types but the height was reduced by 1½-inches (3.8cm). Column change and a three-speed box remained as standard, but a four-speed floor mounted box was offered as an optional extra, at first the travel on this gear change was found to be very spongy and the gearbox noisy, but after these faults were cured the FB became a well-loved family saloon. This standard model, touring London at night must have been pictured late in 1961, the tax disc in the window expiring in January 1962.*

Right: *Photographed around the same time, we see here the super estate version, again in London, in front of what we think is a Rolls-Royce Silver Wraith of around 1948 vintage.*

Above: *Once again examination of Vauxhall's publicity records show that the company were aiming some of their products at very specific markets. One of the markets it identified for its estate car products was the 'country set', and many of the pictures show estate cars on farms, race-courses, stables, golf courses, grouse shoots and so on. Here we see a 'farm setting' for a 1964 Victor FC Model 101 Super Estate. Interior space on the FC models was improved by using curved side windows. The model replaced the FB-Victor in 1964 and remained in production until 1967.*

Left: *Employing a similar body style to the FB Victor, the PB series Cresta and Velox were quite a comparison with the stylish PAs that had gone before. Here we have a PB Velox, pictured in Woburn. It will be noted that this model has a mono-tone finish, plain wheel discs and no chrome flash along the side. In all 87,047 PBs were made, but the Velox was by far the smaller percentage.*

Above: *Giving the impression that a successful couple could enjoy a peaceful weekend in their luxurious HA Viva, this publicity shot shows an SL90 model in an autumnal setting alongside a quiet harbour. Said to be photographed 'Somewhere in Cornwall', the picture shows that the car was finished in Grecian White with a black flash. It was one of the 307,738 HA Viva's built before the company introduced the HB Viva in 1966.*

Right: *I remember walking through the town centre of Holmfirth (near Huddersfield) one Saturday in 1964 on my way to play football at school. Here a young local musician named Roy Castle was playing his trumpet and tap dancing in front of a display stand. The event was to attract attention to the arrival of the new Vauxhall HA Viva, and the whole town (now famous as the setting for* Last Of The Summer Wine*) seemed to be examining this popular little car. Here we see a picture of the estate version, the Bedford Beagle.*

31

Above: *In 1964, and thus within the scope of this book, Vauxhall announced the successor to the PB range, which (at three years) turned out to be very short-lived when compared to the PA. This 1965 Vauxhall Cresta PC saloon is the basic model, as the deluxe model boasted dual headlamps. This car featured what was called 'Coke Bottle' styling, and this was carried on to the FD Victor, which replaced the FC101. It is interesting to note that in its appearance a certain amount of American influence has started to reappear, signifying (perhaps) a response to customer and dealer demand!*

Left: *By contrast, and identified by the twin headlamps and full wheel trims, we now show the PC Cresta Deluxe. The absence of the Velox name from the range at this time meant that just two models were initially introduced in the PC series, but in due course the luxuriously appointed 3,3 litre PC Viscount would come along.*

FB Victor & VX4/90 1961-1964

With almost one third of a million cars produced in the FB Victor range, this 1508cc offering from Luton promised to be a real successor to the 1957 F Type Victors. Launched in 1961, this modest, sober family saloon was designed to appeal to a truly European audience. The gaudy American influence with wrap-round windows, flashy chrome trim and eye-catching features had gone, and the FB emerged as a relatively conventional, almost boring-looking saloon. It was in the same basic mould as the Ford Cortina that would appear a year later in 1962, and the two cars were to become fierce competitors in the years that followed.

Above: *The new FB Victor. Again pictured on an airfield, but with somewhat of a contrast to the picture seen on page 14. Instead of using one of Britain's most modern aircraft as a backdrop, the setting this time emphasises something more traditional. Here we see one of the famous De-Havilland DH82s, which entered service in 1939 and became better known as the 'Tiger Moth' bi-plane. Registered G-ANFC, it is painted bright yellow, whilst the car is a Series I Vauxhall Victor FB Deluxe. Although not shown in any of the views presented, we might mention that the Series I had an oblong rear number plate, but that on the later models was square-shaped within a frame that incorporated the boot handle.*

Top Right: *At the Albert Memorial, erected by Queen Victoria in memory of her late husband and consort Prince Albert, we see one of the new Series I FB Victors. This is the Victor FBE, which was the company's designation for the Deluxe model. The basic model was the FBS, the Super was the FBD whilst the estates were FBW (Super) and FBG (Deluxe).*

Centre Right: *Being a bit on the flippant side, my co-author Rob decided to caption this picture 'underneath the arches' - he's a bit of a Flanagan and Allen fan!!!! Actually this is an assembly line picture of late PA Crestas and early FB Victors, showing this to be a 1962 view. Making this in the middle of what was a transitional period at Vauxhall as new models were coming on stream, and quite possibly towards the very end of the PA production.*

Bottom Right: *This photograph shows an early Deluxe version of the FB Victor, and is included as it shows off the rear-quarters of the model with the rear light clusters and petrol filler clearly seen. You can also just see the discrete V emblems on the wheel discs. Also in the 'showroom' picture, the advertising for the new motorway network is clearly a sign of the times, as is the £450 purchase price on the window of the full-screen Bedford CA van.*

Style-wise the new Vauxhall could easily be considered as an early example of standardised design, featuring simple, uncluttered, yet flowing lines running from the windscreen down the bonnet, to a low full-width radiator grill. The radiator grill had a slight V, and was made up from a series of horizontal chrome bars. The headlamps were positioned at the outer edges of the grill, with lozenge-shaped sidelight/indicator clusters located below.

The flanks of the car were modest and unadorned, save for the name Victor being spelt out in stylised chrome letters on the front wings near the leading edge of the front door. A convex rib ran round the wheel-arches and along the door sills. Another style line was the short convex pressing in the rear wing that lead from the rear tail-light cluster to a vanishing point by the rear wheel arch. The final feature formed a slight lip following the sweep of the boot that ran along the doors just below the windows and disappeared into the leading edge of the front wing. This can be readily seen in the picture above, and if you think about this styling featured you can see that it gave the impression that the famous Vauxhall 'flute' was still alive and doing well.

The basic model in the new FB range was the standard saloon, which came in a choice of six monotone colours, and featured bench seats upholstered in Pewter Grey Vynide. It sold at £510, plus £234 19s 9d purchase tax (adding almost half as much again to the total), making a price of £744 19s 9d. (£8,891). However, for the luxury of a 4-speed floor-change gearbox, the price cost another £17 10s (£209.14). If you wanted something a little bit more up-market, the Victor Super came out at £791 8s 11d (including tax) or £9,456 at today's value. Although it was still plagued with the Vynide seating, this model was offered in a choice of five interior colours.

Externally, the buyer had a choice of 14 body colours set off by the lavish embellishment of stainless steel brightwork around the windows. Then came the Deluxe models, with their interiors furnished in leather upholstery. Mind you Vynide was still used on the seat backs, but the car was given the luxury of individual front seats. A choice of five special duo-tone colour schemes was available for the insides, and tufted rayon carpeting adorned the floor. Further 'luxury features' included a screenwasher and a powerful heater.

Externally the Deluxe had the same brightwork and stainless steel trim found on the Super, but it also had V badges on the wheel embellishers. The most striking feature was the range of colours, no less than 14 single tones and seven two-tone schemes. In the two-tone schemes, the roof and rear window pillars were painted a contrasting colour to the main body paint, and a very small number were supplied with an experimental black leather cloth finish. Including tax, the Deluxe cost £847 1s 5d (£10,122), and once again the 4-speed box was available as a £17 10s optional extra.

For the sum of £861.13s 0 d (£10,297), a really attractive estate car could be purchased as a factory-built model. Based on the specification of the Super saloon, the FBW estate featured a 45.5 cu. ft. load space with easy access by means of a large, counter-balanced tailgate. This tailgate featured a slight inward curve on its bottom corners which, when in the closed position, allowed the tailgate to fit neatly round the rear light clusters. The load space area measured 65 inches by 54 1/4 inches, and featured load deck rubbing strips of a plastic material set in chrome strips. A bench seat came as standard, but individual front seats could be specified as an optional extra, and whilst these were popular few buyers opted to have the floor-mounted gearbox lever.

Top Right: *Here we have a study of the family resemblance between the Series I FB Victor and the PB Velox in the background. This view dates from 1963 and illustrates the striking likeness between the four-cylinder and six-cylinder models that were produced at Luton at that time, yet a feature that had been missing from the Vauxhall range since 1957. Here the famous race-horse trainer (Sir) Gordon Richards sits in his Super Estate chatting with a stable-hand.*

Centre Right: *As mentioned elsewhere, the development of standard models for use in competitions had been something that Vauxhall had found to be especially useful in attracting new custom. Here the new VX4/90 demonstrates its potential in a snow-bound section of the 32nd Rallye Automobile Monte-Carlo. The year is 1963, and an abundance of external lighting is clearly seen, making quite a difference from those oil lights seen in the earlier pictures of Vauxhall cars!*

Bottom Right: *However, the VX4/90 was not just a rally car, and Vauxhall marketed it as a 'town and country saloon' - a role it took to like a duck to water! Seen crossing a ford in the Cotswolds, this Series II VX4/90, clearly shows the side flash that immediately identified the larger engined 1594cc car!*

Above: *The Canadian/North American version of the FB Victor, was named the Envoy and resembled the later model VX4/90. This picture pre-dates the modified VX4/90 and dates from 1963.*

Vauxhall also offered a new 'top of the range' car with the VX4/90, in which the designation VX referred to Vauxhall, the 4 meant four cylinders, and the 90 indicated the top speed. One leading classic car magazine later described this car as 'The hot one, with twin carbs, 71bhp engine, individual front seats, servo front discs, four-on-the-floor, a different grille and colour side-flashes. Will do 90mph: plenty of noise though, and a Cortina GT will blow it away across country.' In contrasting the VX4/90 to Ford's Cortina, the writer ignores the basic marketing concept that Vauxhall were applying to their flagship car. Basically few owners would ever have really wanted a car that could achieve really high performance, but in the image conscious days of the Swinging Sixties, first impressions were what counted.

Ford had found, to very good effect, what a successful rally car could mean to its sales of standard saloons in the 1950s, and the MkI and MkII Zephyr rallying successes really did have a knock-on effect for ordinary sales. Even sales of the little Ford Anglia 105E were to show a measured improvement, thanks to the car's success in competitions.

Vauxhall, acutely aware of the importance of this facet of sales, knew it had to have a 'performance' car in the range. Using a high compression engine with an aluminium cylinder head and a twin carburettor, the VX4/90 developed 15bhp more than the standard FB Victor and was rated at 1508cc.

Because of its 'sporty' image, the VX4/90 was always sold with the all-synchromesh four-speed floor-change gearbox and had the features mentioned in the review above, but it also had revised suspension, a more comfortable foam-filled upholstery, screenwash, and a rev counter for those who really wanted to show off. Externally it could be easily recognised by the different radiator grill, its 'T' shaped rear lamp clusters and the aforementioned side flash that was also meant to convey an impression of the Vauxhall flute. Earlier models had a slight step in the flash, with the portion on the rear door and rear wings being wider than it was on the front door and wings.

The VX4/90 was obviously the most expensive model in the FB range, with a basic price of £665 plus tax at £306 0s 7d, making a total outlay of £971 0s 7d (£11,604). This was a substantial sum for what was basically an image car, but it did prove to be extremely popular, although the exact production figures are not available. Improvements to the FB range of Vauxhall Victors included the introduction of a 1594cc engine in 1963, which was basically pre-empting the introduction of the FC Victor (known as the Victor 101) a year later. The same engine change affected the VX4/90 giving it an 85 bhp rating. Also in readiness for the FC range, a final rash of improvements to the FB were introduced early in 1964, at which time servo front discs, a new facia and larger clutches became available.

It is also worth mentioning that the FB series might have been developed as a rear-engined car! Consulting engineers had been extensively studying the Chevrolet Corvair, with a view to introducing this for the European market, where it would have taken on cars like Renault's Dauphine and the ubiquitous Volkswagen. In fact Vauxhall extensively tested an FB against a Beetle, and the FB came out on top in most respects. It would have taken some getting used to, and one suspects that it would not have done particularly well as an export model! Fortunately, Vauxhall decided to resist both the American and European influence and produced a very British car. Its quiet styling, and loss of the American look did not go unnoticed, but it certainly found approval from the new General Motors president John Gordon, when he visited Luton in 1959.

Before concluding with the subject of the FB Victor, it is well worth mentioning a little about the export market Vauxhall had developed. Driven by Government in the second half of the 1940s, following the 'Export or Die' campaign, Vauxhall had found itself entering new markets in its attempts to bring in that much-needed foreign currency. Traditional markets like the Empire (later Commonwealth) countries had long been established, but new opportunities presented themselves, and the expansion of the Luton plant (and later the new factories at Dunstable and Ellesmere Port) reflected this factor. The year 1964 saw the massive total of 342,873 Vauxhalls and Bedfords being produced, with the popular little HA Viva being a big seller. The Viva was to do exceptionally well in Canada, building on the strength of earlier imported Vauxhalls, and it had the distinction of becoming the top-selling imported car in the land of the Maple Leaf.

When I was working with David Brown Tractors in the 1960s, we found that the Canadian market (except in Quebec) was very pro-British, and we could sell our tractors far more easily than the Americans could sell theirs. To an extent the same was also true with saloon cars, and Vauxhall certainly did very well despite the nearness of the General Motors plants in the USA. All of which brings us back to a variant of the FB, which was little known in Britain (although I have seen a picture of one of these cars in a right-hand version in Ireland). The car concerned was the FB Envoy (saloon version) and the Sherwood (estate car). The basic difference in these two models, when compared to the Victors, was mainly styling and detail changes, and these are evident from a comparison of the pictures.

Above and Below: *Although we could only find one picture of the Envoy saloon, we did uncover these two illustrations of the Sherwood Estate, and we hope that you will appreciate the chance to compare these with the British offering. We know that the Sherwood sold into Canada, and as suggested in the text at least one was first registered in the Irish Republic. Does anyone know where else these cars went, if anywhere? The Vauxhall Epic, another export model, based on Vauxhall's HA Viva has proved a little elusive also, but we at least know that it went to Australia, Canada, USA, France and Belgium. As the Epic and Sherwood/Envoy were contemporaries of one another, did the FB derived cars get to the same destinations? Vauxhall's records are not clear on the subject, but someone surely knows the answer!*

Above: *The Viva HA, the reliable small saloon introduced for the 1960s 'family market'. Its success and popularity can easily be determined by the 303,738 built between 1963 and 1966.*

HA VIVA 1953-1966

September 1963 was to see Vauxhall launch its first small saloon car in nearly 30 years, with the introduction of the Vauxhall Viva HA. The need for a small saloon was becoming essential to the Vauxhall range, at a time when the working classes were changing from public transport to private car ownership. Essentially the motorcycle combination had proved to be the entry point for the family market, but the great success of the Morris 1000, Austin A30/A35, the small Rootes Group cars and Ford's Anglia/Popular/Prefect 100E and the Anglia 105E had shown that here was a market that really could not be ignored by Vauxhall. The main problem was that Luton was already being worked to capacity, and the output on the larger cars showed no sign of diminishing. In 1955 the Bedford truck production had to be moved to a new plant at Dunstable, and this plant was also working to capacity as the millionth Bedford was produced in 1958. The following year Luton turned out the 2-millionth Vauxhall, and there was literally no capacity for a small car.

To address the problem of capacity, and given the incentive of selective financial assistance, the company announced that it was to open a new plant at Hooton, near Ellesmere Port on the south side of the River Mersey. Located on the site of a former RAF base, the site offered good communications by road, rail and sea, and of course it was also in one of the Economic Development Areas. The Vauxhall Directors considered many other alternatives, but the Cheshire site won out, and it was decided that it would be the base for the manufacture of the new 'H Concept' car. Construction work began in August 1960, and the first Viva rolled off the specially-built Ellesmere Port plant in August 1964. However, the success of the small BMC and Ford saloons (especially the Mini), prompted Vauxhall to commence the production of some Viva saloons at Luton in September 1963, just in time for the forthcoming Motor Show.

Another essential requirement for the new saloon, was the potential to develop into car-derived commercial vehicles. Light vans, pick-up trucks and small estate cars were all planned around the 1057cc four-cylinder engine. This strong little engine had a large bore and a short stroke, a down-draught single Solex carburettor, and produced 44bhp giving a top speed of around 80mph. Transmission was by an all synchromesh four-speed gearbox, using a short floor-mounted gear stick. This gave much faster changes through the gears, and thus made it ideal for new drivers!

Originally just the basic and Deluxe saloons were offered, and as the accompanying picture of the launch shows, these were offered respectively at £527.7s.11d (£5,428) and £566.1s.3d (£5,829) including purchase tax. Without this tax the cars cost £436 (£4,490) and £468 (£4,820). This means at today's prices the Government would rake in around £1,000 for each car produced, which wasn't a bad return on their financial assistance when one considers that 100,000 Vivas had been sold within ten months of the car's launch - that was a cool £100 million in today's values going back into the Chancellor's coffers. The fairly solid Labour votes from the car workers employed at the plant wouldn't have harmed Harold Wilson (himself a Merseyside MP) or his new Government either.

Top Right: *Styling of the Vauxhall Viva (and all the firm's new cars at that time), would have begun life in the Design Department. Using sketches, mocked-up photographs (pictures of parts of vehicles superimposed onto drawings) and clay models such as the one shown here, and a new car slowly comes to life.*

Centre Right: *Moving on from the clay model, we see the next stage with a HA Viva made in fibre-glass. Whether this view represents a 'final design', a styling development of the car, or its next stage in life as the HB Viva, we have no idea. However, a clue may well be gained from the pictures on the walls around the car, as these look very much like the embryo HB model. It is therefore likely that both these pictures refer to the metamorphism of the Viva, rather than its genesis, but whatever the case, the original HA Viva design concept would have started off in life like this; designs, sketches, mock-ups, wooden models, clay models, fibre-glass shells and finally completed cars. Much more work would then follow in the Engineering Department before the model was ever put on general release!*

Bottom Right: *Talking of general release, here we see Vauxhall's then Director of Sales, Geoff Welby announcing the new Viva! Complete with attractive models dressed in diamante swimsuit's, a blonde model holds a card pronouncing a cost of £468 (£566.1s.3d with Tax) for the Deluxe model, whilst a brunette holds a similar board for the basic model proclaiming a cost of just £436 (£527.7s.11d with Tax). A collection of photographs showing pretty girls and new cars would undoubtedly make the basis for a best-selling car book, but would our wives tolerate our drooling over the attractive models inside? Sorry dear I was talking about the cars, honestly!*

Top Left: *The Viva got its name from a fellow Yorkshireman (sorry to wave the White Rose chaps, but we are apt to be a bit patriotic up North). This particular Yorkshireman was one William Swallow, who became Vauxhall's Managing Director in 1961. It fell to him to chose a name that suited the little car, and the one that he eventually devised conjured quite up a bit of Latin flare. The Viva name carried on through various series in the Vauxhall range until 1979 when the HC Viva was phased out - meantime around 1.6 million cars wore Swallow's Viva badge!*

Centre Left: *The bright mouldings on the side show this to be a HA Viva Deluxe. It is powered by a 1057cc engine based on its German cousin, the Opel Kadett.*

Bottom Left: *As mentioned earlier, there was one member of the Viva family that was not particularly well-known in the UK, namely the Epic. This was primarily an export version of the HA Viva, and it was built both in Luton and at the Liege plant in Belgium, and pictured here in a publicity picture taken in a snowy Scandinavian setting.*

Right: *The sheer export potential of the HA Viva can be readily appreciated from this picture taken at Ellesmere Port showing dozens of right-hand drive models awaiting shipment overseas.*

Even the basic Viva offered spacious accommodation for four passengers, but it was a bit pinched with five adults. The boot offered quite a good 10 cubic feet of load space, achieved by the square boxy shape of the car. However, some of the reviewers of the time failed to appreciate that Vauxhall were actually promoting a low-cost entry point for the new motorist, and criticised the car as being 'Spartan'.

Heaven forbid anyone should criticise, and for me the Viva was certainly a step up from the BSA, Ariel or Triumph motorbikes and the draughty sidecars that I had to endure on family trips to the seaside. Huddersfield to Scarborough or Blackpool in one uncle's basic Viva was far better than the same journey in another uncle's motorcycle combination. Anyway, to resolve the criticisms Vauxhall did introduce a better appointed SL saloon ready for the summer of 1965.

The Viva's dimensions were an overall length of 11ft 12in x 4ft 11in x 4ft 5in high. The turning circle was 29ft 6in. They were painted in a new 'Magic Mirror' acrylic lacquer paint, and came in a choice of Grecian White, Storm Grey, Meteor Blue or Calypso Red. The Deluxe came in the same basic colours, but also black, Pacific Blue, Jade Green or Cavalry Fawn.

The SL and SL90 Viva models, with their more luxurious appointments, featured a colour scheme with a contrasting flash along their sides which was surrounded by a chrome border. In all some 11,794 SL and SL90s were built, but this was a tiny figure compared with the other 309,538 Viva saloons that were built before the HB Viva was introduced in 1966.

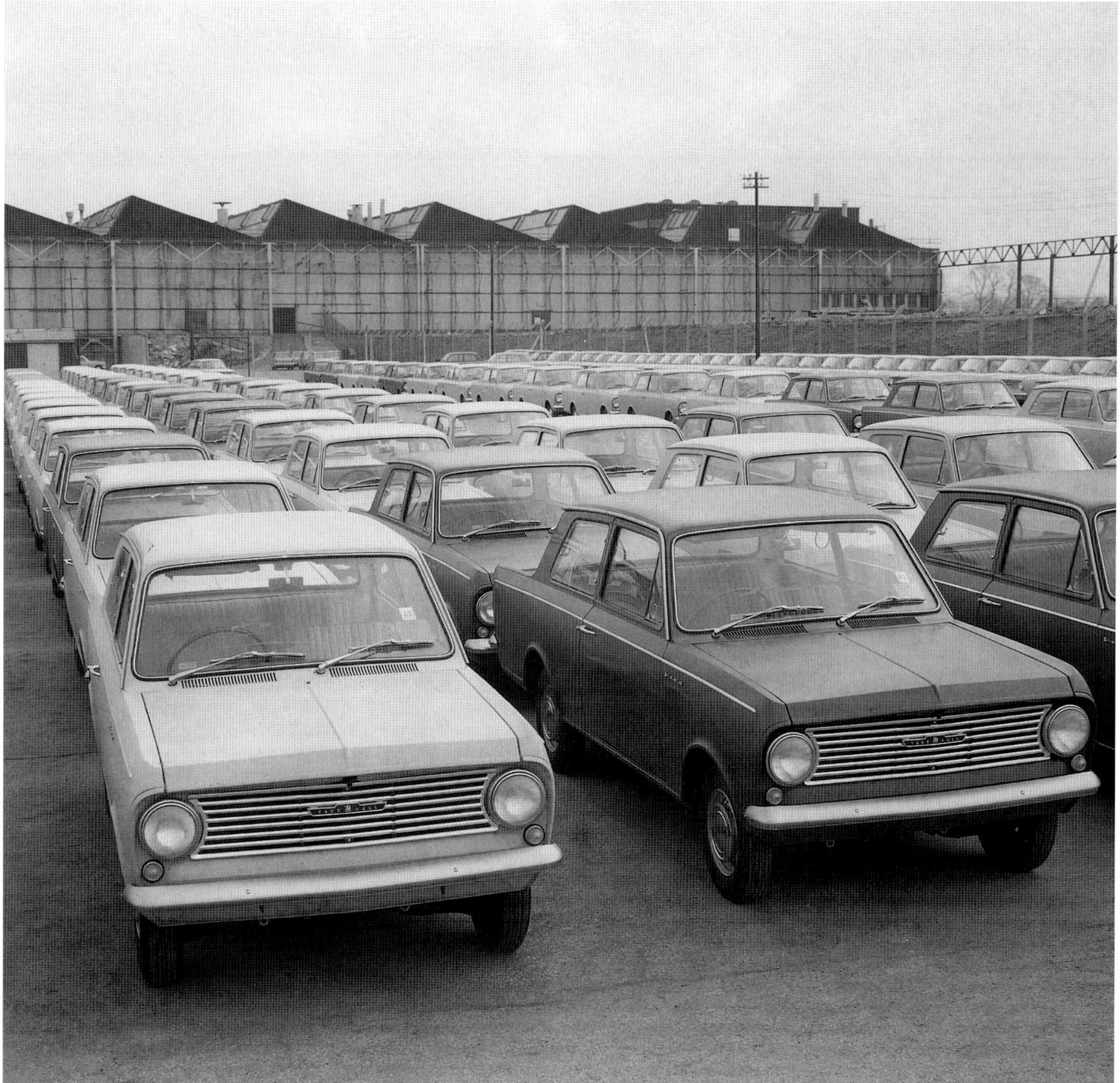

In August of 1964 the HA range was expanded with a car-derived 6-cwt van, the first such car-based light commercial produced by Vauxhall since the PC Bedford van had been phased out in favour of the 10-/12-cwt CA in 1952. This was later offered as an 8-cwt van, and finally in the 10-cwt capacity in 1972 to cater for the increasing loads that small commercials were expected to carry. The subject of the HA van, and its brethren in the Bedford range is covered in a **Nostalgia Road** book from Trans-Pennine, which is entitled *Bedford Light Commercials 0f the 1950s & '60s*. Coverage of the HA van will not therefore be given in this present volume, but we must consider two passenger-carrying derivatives of the van.

From the outset the new HA van body could be purchased with rear side windows, and one issue of the *Bedford Magazine* showed how an electrical company had created illuminated adverts to fit behind the 'glass panels', but the idea never really caught on. What did take off was the rather attractive 'estate car' version of the HA, which was known as the Bedford Beagle. This was in production from 1963 to 1967, and it was often sold for a dual role, i.e.: a commercial vehicle during the day, and a family saloon in the evenings or weekends.

By 1965 the firm of Martin Walter, were busily converting the Bedford CA chassis into a very practical camper. With the arrival of the HA van, they found they could offer a smaller Dormobile model. Fitted with an elevating roof and called the Roma, the small Dormobile was equipped to carry two adults and a child. However, it also had an awning that could be fitted to provide extended accommodation when the tailgate was in the open position. The Roma filled a very interesting niche in the market, being the first modern camper van aimed primarily at married couples rather than family groups.

Top Left: *The Martin Walter prototype HA dormobile seen here in February 1965. Although the Viva, the Beagle and their light commercial equivalents shared many identical components, not everything was the same. One example would be the van doors, which looked like those on the car but were actually taller, another major difference was the gearbox and prop shaft.*

Centre Left: *The attraction of a light commercial van, which could also double as a family saloon, was a well-tried concept by the time that the HA came along. Ford with its 100E series, Austin (with the A35 Countryman) and Morris with the 1000 Traveller had shown this to be quite a lucrative market - especially with the small businessman or commercial traveller (rep). This internal view of the HA shows the load-space area with rear seat down, with period electrical equipment in the back and Vauxhall photographer Norman Page in the front.*

Bottom Left: *Another market for the Beagle was found in both agricultural circles. As this picture seems to suggest, this 1057cc estate was quite capable of carrying milk churns (presumably if the milk tanker forgot to call), or for going shopping in!*

PB Velox & Cresta 1962-1965

After the wonderful, ostentatious and (to a degree) extravagant PA series Velox and Cresta, many commentators expressed surprise at the unveiling of the PB range that succeeded them. The launch of the new range of six-cylinder cars showed that Vauxhall were now offering a large, but quite orthodox looking saloon. The only thing that the PA and PB series had visually in common were the Velox and Cresta names. Again the Cresta was furnished with the lion's share of extra equipment, but it cost around £100 (£1,088) more than the Velox.

In appearance the two new large cars had a lot of family resemblance to the smaller FB model Victor. True, the Velox and the Cresta had a much more 'gutsy' look about them. Whereas the Victor had gentle, soft flowing lines to the bonnet and boot, the Velox and the Cresta had a defined edge to theirs.

Above: *Contrasting views between the two six-cylinder PB models, at the top we see a Velox, whilst a Cresta occupies the lower position. This interesting view enables us to contrast the front and rear aspect of the PB saloons, whilst immediate differences like the wheel trims and tyres are also seen. This view was taken during a publicity run to the Scottish Highlands.*

The Victor's boot also had an attractive curve, but the six-cylinder models had a pronounced chamfer to their counterbalanced boot. Just below the lid, horizontal lamp clusters were mounted in a lozenge-shaped housing. Both cars had fine chrome work, and a notable feature was the rear bumper, which had a central recess to accommodate the number plate. On the Cresta a fine chrome band ran along the top corner of the rear wings, crossed the doors, then passed along the front wings to finish at a peak in the wing a few inches above the headlamps.

The headlamps themselves were set outside the radiator grill, which was made up from a series of horizontal chrome bars and one singular vertical band in the centre. Another feature, the sidelight and indicator cluster, is readily seen from the picture above. Mounted in the bottom of the wing, just above the bumper, they were more readily observed by other road users. Vauxhall described these as an improved safety feature, which they were, but as the cars aged they were badly affected by mud and debris that was thrown up from the road. If this built up behind them and caused rusting, and in the case of a good friend (who shall remain nameless) it cost him a couple of points on his licence. When travelling down the cobbled Alder Street, in Huddersfield late at night, the nearside cluster in his 11 year old Velox, dropped free - unfortunately he was following a police car at the time.

Above: *How things have changed, especially in road transport, and no longer do travellers bound for the North East of Scotland have to endure the car ferries of the Firth of Forth. Here we see a PB Cresta coming off the ferry* William Wallace *at North Queensferry en-route for a photo-shoot in the Highlands. The ferries across the Firth had been developed from a haphazard rowing boat service by the North British Railway who instituted a steam-powered ferry service in 1850 to connect with passenger trains running from Edinburgh to the north. The ferries were designed by Thomas (later Sir Thomas) Bouch who was then commissioned to design a railway bridge. Work started in 1878, but after Bouch's bridge over the Firth of Tay collapsed in a ferocious storm on 31st December 1879, the work was suspended. A new design was drawn up by John Fowler and Benjamin Baker, it was opened in March 1890 and is seen here dominating this picture.*

Top Right: *Around four and a half miles south of Hungerford on the A338 road, an early PB Velox reaches the crossroads of the Marlborough road. The sylvan surroundings of the Berkshire countryside, the quiet road, and the lovely old road sign bring back memories of days when vehicles were individual and a journey was a great adventure!*

Centre Right: *This view captures a little recorded aspect of daily life in Vauxhall's works at Luton, with cars coming off the end of the production line. Here we see the final inspection process being undertaken on a batch of early PB Velox and PB Cresta models before their delivery to the dealers or despatch to the docks for export. The many checks that were undertaken here were quite essential, as they ensured that the final quality of the build met the standards set down by the company.*

Bottom Right: *Full six-seater comfort and their powerful 6-cylinder engines help explain why the PB Vauxhall models were well-liked by taxi operators. In many ways the Vauxhall PB range proved to be very practical taxis and hire cars, offering a degree of luxury at a reasonable price. Quite a number were also used by firms operating funeral services and wedding cars. It is not surprising therefore that black was one of the standard paint schemes offered by Vauxhall, what is more it should be noted that a number of firms also offered a hearse conversion to the six-cylinder Vauxhalls. This is a subject that has never been covered in a British motoring publication, and a **Nostalgia Road** book on hearses and funeral cars is currently planned for release in the year 2002.*

The cars were 15 feet 1 inch long and were carried on Firestone 5.90 x 14-inch tubeless tyres. They were powered by six-in-line engines of a square configuration, which had an 82.6mm bore and stroke that gave a displacement of 2651cc. They were also fitted with a single Zenith 42VNT carburettor. This continued the Vauxhall reputation for producing a powerful saloon, and again the six-cylinder cars were used in a large number of competitions, including the Monte-Carlo Rally, but it was as a top flight family saloon or businessman's car that they really excelled.

A manual three-speed gearbox was the standard option, but automatic transmission was provided with the Hydra-Matic gearbox which was available as an 'optional extra' on either car. Interestingly, in addition to the normal park, neutral, drive, and low positions on standard automatic gearboxes, the Hydra-Matic had a further position marked 'S'. When this position was selected it held the second gear up to a maximum speed of 59mph and changed down at 52mph. Overdrive was also available as an option!

Suspension on the new PB cars was by independent coil springs and wishbones, with telescopic dampers at the front and half-elliptic leaf springs and automatic dampers at the rear. The brakes were Lockheed hydraulic with vacuum servo assistance, with disc brakes at the front and drum brakes at the rear.

Above and Below: *These two pictures clearly illustrate the external changes that were incorporated in the top car within the PB range. This executive model, known as The Radford Cresta, was an official conversion undertaken by the London-based coachbuilders Harold Radford, and was marketed to well-heeled members of the general public between October 1963 and 1964. (Some were also produced for military use as 'staff cars', and a batch were still being exported to the Middle-East as late as the spring of 1965). The exterior of the Radford car was finished in a special paint, and at the rear it featured a silver panel between the tail lights. A full folding sun-roof, bumper over-riders, dual headlamps and a new style of wheel trim were all featured in the 'extra' appointments of the PB Radford. However, it was the lavish interior where the car showed its 'executive' flair, not least in the glass 'chauffeur's screen' between the front and rear seats. Rear seat passengers enjoyed luxurious extras such as reading lamps and fold-down 'picnic tables'.*

As mentioned previously, the Cresta was very well equipped, and featured a deep padded top to the facia panel, with a Burr Walnut band embellishing both it and the glove-box locker below. A clock was mounted between the padded sun visors, and even the steering wheel had a padded cross bar. Other refinements included a chrome horn ring on the steering wheel, map pockets in the front footwells on either side of the car, provision for seat belts, and a powerful heater/de-mister unit.

Externally the Cresta was identified by the extra chrome trim and by the provision of fog and spot lamps. The Cresta was easily recognised at a distance due to the fact that it was offered in one of six two-tone colour schemes and by the thin white wall tyres it wore.

Improvements were made to the PB range in 1964 when a 3.3 litre engine was fitted to both models, giving 128hp. A floor-mounted four-speed gear change became available as an optional extra, but the most visual change was the introduction of a new full-width radiator grill. Also in 1964 Vauxhall were able to offer estate car versions of the PB Velox and Cresta by Martin Walter. As will be recalled, this Folkestone-based company had begun converting the E-Type Velox in 1957, and they would also go on to be chosen for the conversion to the PC range when it was introduced in 1965. Yet this seemed a strange decision in light of the fact that the company had already begun a production line build of a Victor estate at Luton.

The Velox was launched with a price of £822 (£8,945) for the standard saloon or £955 (£10,393) for the Hydra-Matic, The standard Cresta cost £919 (£10,001) and £1,052 (£11,448) for the Hydra-Matic, The PB range remained in production for a relatively short time, as the Velox was withdrawn at the end of 1964, and the PB Cresta superseded by the PC Cresta in the summer of 1965. Yet in the short period of time they were in production, a total of 87,047 cars were produced, and this outstripped the 81,841 of the PA Velox and Cresta models, and almost reached the massive total of 91,923 cars produced in the PASX Velox/PADX Cresta range that the PB Cresta/Velox replaced.

However, their brief lifespan may well have been due to the fact that they were nowhere near as visually appealing as the PA models that had preceded them. In a confidential memo sent to Vauxhall dealers in February 1964, ahead of the PB refinements of that year, the company were promising that a new, exciting 6-cylinder car was already under development for launch the following year. The motoring press began to circulate rumours that a new space age car was being promised by Vauxhall, and confidential preview brochures released late in 1964 showed that a radically improved and more stylish car using the 3294cc power unit was just around the corner. This was to be the PC series, and although it falls outside the remit of this book's time span, we do spend some time covering these cars at the end of the book, as their development definitely falls within the period under discussion.

A 1965 article in the motoring press which asked, 'Did Vauxhall Get It Wrong' alluded to the styling of the PB series, and suggested that a luxury car should not have had a basic styling that could be found on the mid-range family car like the FB Victor. Mind you, to take that argument a step forward, if you looked closely enough, you could even see a distinct likeness to the front end of the boxy little HA Viva.

The fact that Ford had changed from its extremely stylish Consul Classic to the Cortina suggests that there was a certain vogue for the boxy approach in the early-1960s, but was this for the better? For this writer at least, the PB really had lost a great deal of ground that had been captured by the PAs, which had set Vauxhall so far apart from the other six-cylinder luxury cars then being made in Britain. Probably the most reasonable comment on the subject was made by *Classic & Sportscar* in a 1993 supplement, which kindly described the PB range as a 'reskinned six (which) looks like an overgrown FB Victor.'

Mind you this was still in a time that anything produced at Luton sold, and sold in large quantities to boot. The change from public transport to private car ownership had grown out of all proportion to the national economic growth, but it undoubtedly had a great deal to do with the massive reduction in public transport, in a period when the infamous Dr. Richard Beeching wielded his 'Axe' and decimated British Railways. In the year his decimation began, 1964, Vauxhall achieved its all-time high of 342,873 vehicles, an aggregate of six and a half thousand cars a week. Perhaps these figures speak for themselves, and suggest that the PB was just another step on the road to raising the standard!

Below: *One part of the PB range that had a really stylish appearance, was the Martin Walter estate car conversion, which looked just like a production model. In itself this suggests that there was little wrong with the PB's front end appearance, and that it was basically the back-end that was at fault. By contrast the back end of the estate suggested a certain harmony that was not achieved on the earlier six-cylinder estate conversions (where the back end looked very much like an after-thought). The long association between Vauxhall/Bedford and the Folkestone firm of Martin Walter is part of a unique story, and one which needs much deeper consideration. As will be appreciated from this book, the story goes back quite a way and carried on not only through the estate car conversions, but also on Dormobile crew buses, 'camper vans' and ambulances based on the CA chassis. Yet Martin Walter did much more, and the Vauxhall archive contains many unusual prototype pictures with Martin Walter bodies on Luton-built chassis. Included in these views are pictures of a school bus based on the Bedford VAS chassis. However, much of the vital information on the Vauxhall-Walter association has been lost over the years, and this is an oversight we would like to correct. If any reader can help with information, we'd be delighted to hear from them!*

FC Victor 101 & VX/490 1964-1967

Although we are now approaching the cut-off date for this book (having considered the two decades of post-war Vauxhall production), the company made two important introductions just before the end of 1964. Although several of the vehicles featured in the pages that follow actually post date 1964, the models themselves are an integral part of our story.

The first of these was the Vauxhall Victor 101FC, which was introduced in October 1964 to replace the FB Victor. It was available in two bodyshells, offering either a four-door saloon or a five-door estate. The range of models offered on these two types was much wider, and in total six different cars were available. The range started with a basic saloon (the FCS), which was launched with a £678 (£6,983) price tag. For this modest price you got a 4-door family saloon in a choice of six body colours, with seating for four to five passengers on front and rear bench seats.

Above: *Showing a distinct improvement on the FB Victor range, the new FC series looked a much more stylish car than its predecessor. This view shows the style of the anodised aluminium radiator grill on the 1964-1966 Victor 101, before it was redesigned in September 1966. The FCD Victor 101 Super was sold at a price of £708 (£7,101) when it was first introduced in saloon car form in October 1964.*

The upholstery used on the basic model was Vynide (horribly sticky stuff on a hot sunny day), and the floor had the luxury of fitted rubber mats (which were slippy in wet weather). These appointments were complimented by a single sun visor for the driver, a single tone horn and column gear change. Mind you, if you wanted to splash out on an optional extra or two you could get individual front seats and a floor-mounted gear stick. If you had £708 (£7,292) to spend, you could move up a step to the FCD, otherwise known as the Super Saloon.

This was slightly better appointed than the basic model, and had bright-work in the form of anodised aluminium strips. Inside the floors were carpeted, whilst the facia panel was covered in a padded material. Courtesy lights were another luxury, and these were automatically operated by switches in the doors. Oh, and by the way, the front seat passenger could now put away their sunglasses, as a second visor was provided. There was a choice of nine single tone body colours.

The Victor 101 Deluxe (code FCE) benefited from even more refinement, most noticeably the upholstery which used a material called Ambla. If this wasn't enough, you could get leather furnishing as an optional extra. The bench seat (standard on the other models) was replaced by two thickly padded single seats on the Deluxe version. Arm-rests were fitted to the doors, and beneath the thick cut-pile carpet a sound insulating material was fitted to the floor. A heater-defroster, windscreen washer, dual horns and twin sun visors all came as standard. Externally new wheel embellishers and chrome hub caps were fitted and drip mouldings were made from anodised aluminium. Floor-mounted gear change was available, but as an optional extra. The Deluxe cost just £763 (£7,859) and came in a choice of seven single or five two-tone colours. These two tone colours were applied in the same way as the early PA Cresta saloons, with the second colour being applied to the roof panel and luggage compartment.

The sum of £775 (£7,982.50p) bought you a very practical estate car (the FCW) that had a 51.6cu ft of load space. The dimension of the cargo area was 69in x 53½in with the rear seats folded down. A one-piece, top-hinged tailgate with counter-balanced torsion beams, provided a wide entry aperture. This was a useful feature that endeared the estate to several police forces and ambulance services. Equipment was the same as the Super saloon, but the Super estate version was also available in a choice of four two-tone shades. A second estate car (the FCG) carried the name Victor Deluxe Estate, and had the luxurious appointments of the Deluxe saloon. It came in six single tone colours and four two-tone shades and carried the 1964 price of £859 (£8,847).

The sixth and final car in the range was the superb VX4/90 saloon. Offering higher performance from its 1595cc 4-cylinder engine, the VX4/90 developed 85.5bhp in twin carburettor form. A four-speed gear box was fitted as standard, but 'Power-Glide' automatic transmission became an option on all Victor models in May 1965. A slight fault in the VX4/90 led to a number of prematurely worn clutches, and as a consequence Vauxhall redesigned the clutch housing and began fitting these in October 1965. Retrospective fitting was carried out by the dealerships on cars in service, if the owners reported a problem, but not everybody experienced trouble. At the same time the air filter was replaced, following a redesign to cope with below par performance.

The VX4/90 had several features that set it apart from the other models sharing the same bodyshell. The first was the stylish radiator grill and the side flash in a contrasting colour to the body paint. The VX4/90 carried its own distinctive badge, initially fitted on the off-side corner of the boot lid, this was later moved to a far more prominent position on front wings. As I recall, the badge was also something of a collectors item by unscrupulous schoolboys with screwdrivers.

Above: *This car was the prototype FC Vauxhall VX4/90, and it featured in a large number of publicity pictures ranging from mountain locations to 'beach shots'. It will be seen that the prototype does not have a side flash, which was a feature of the production model, and it has a different coloured roof panel but this does not appear on the production models. The car was registered in London to partially disguise the fact it was a prototype, as it attracted less attention than a Luton registration.*

Below: *Like the six-cylinder PC range, the four-cylinder FC models benefited from an increased cabin space as a result of the pronounced curvature of the doors and window glass. This added internal space gave much more comfortable accommodation for four passengers, and it wasn't all that cramped when five adults were carried. In this 1964 picture the obligatory female model appears once again, this time wearing less revealing clothing and something that is more appropriate to the wintry weather.*

Above and Below: *Comparisons of the production line VX4/90 (above) and the prototype (ALP 450B) seen below. The pictures show the stylish lines of one of the new high-performance six-cylinder cars. It will be noted that the production model also carries the new side flash, but this is missing from the prototype. The prototype was actually given individual front seats, a floor-mounted gear change on a four-speed gear box, and a new facia panel with different instrumentation for the instruments. The difference this made in the driving of the car, was instantly recognised and with variations the revised layout was applied to the production line VX4/90s. These cars also featured a four-dial instrument package that looked quite impressive. This package included a water/oil-pressure gauge, a tachometer, a speedometer (with mileage recorder and trip meter), and an ammeter (with ignition, generator and indicator direction lights). The car seen in the upper picture (taken outside the prestigious Park Lane Hotel), can be readily identified as one of the earlier production models by the fact that the VX4/90 badge is positioned on the rear window pillar, but this was later positioned on the rear wings instead.*

Internally the VX4/90 was the most luxurious of the FC models, and consequently this gave it the edge over many of its contemporaries. A test report in the *Motor* magazine commented, 'the quality of a Rover or Wolseley at the price of a Ford.' Unlike the other models in the range, where a four-speed gear box was only an option, on the VX4/90 it came as standard with a floor-mounted gear lever.

The dashboard also had a different instrument panel and facia, with a four cowled circular instrument panel (this was up-dated by means of a polished walnut-effect finish from 1966 onwards). Because of the advantageous price (when compared to contemporary cars of a similar type), the VX4/90 found itself being adopted by several police forces. Naturally it did well with those forces who already had an allegiance to the Vauxhall marque, but it also sold to many new ones as well.

Progressive improvements were made on the flagship of the range until the FC was replaced by the overhead cam engined models of the FD series in August 1967. Although this model is slightly outside the scope of the book, the FD VX4/90 was the first company car that I was ever allowed to use during my time with the David Brown Corporation - this included making several official trips to the Luton works. It certainly made a change from my own entirely unreliable Austin A35 Countryman (1959 vintage), or the Huddersfield Corporation double deck Daimler CVG6s that I was more commonly obliged to use.

In August 1965 a different numbering system was adopted by Vauxhall, and this affected all the Victor models. The following year saw a new anodised aluminium grill being fitted across the range, and the addition of bright sill moulding below the doors of the deluxe models. Other improvements included re-designed seating and improved interior trim, and bigger front brake cylinders. A nagging problem, with water penetration in some cars was resolved by improved weatherstrip sealing and a substantial development in the technology used to make the glass screens. The estate cars also benefited from the fitting of larger wheels and tyres, and this alleviated several road handling problems that drivers had reported on the earlier models when they were driven fully loaded in poor conditions.

Modest price increases were natural during the life of the FC Victors, but given that this was a time of financial instability in Britain, the cost of the cars did not keep up to the level of inflation. There was therefore a gradual reduction in the real price of the FC range over the period, a factor that was achieved by Vauxhall's continual investment in modern manufacturing facilities. By the time that the series came to its end in August 1967, the basic FCS saloon cost £721 (£6,489), whilst the Super was listed as £771 (£6.939) and the Deluxe at £807 (£7,263). The estate versions cost £847 (£7,623) and £911 (£8,199), and the VX4/90 £927 (£8,343). Taking the basic car as an example, we see that the price had actually increased by £43 but in today's terms, the price was actually £494 less, and besides that the model purchased in 1967 was a substantial improvement on that introduced three years earlier.

That the FC Victor provided a range of popular saloon cars and estates can be demonstrated by the production figure between October 1964 and August 1967, as 219,814 Victors and 13,449 VX4/90s were produced before the FD series was launched.

Above: *Versatile in either the role of a comfortable family saloon car, or as a two-seat load carrier offering 51.7 cubic feet capacity, the FCW Victor 101 was an exceptionally versatile car. The estate was available in any one of five single tone colours, or one of four two-tone body colours as shown here. From these pictures it will be noted that the second colour was basically applied to the roof panel, and the upper half of the real tailgate.*

Below: *Showing the dividing line in the two colours, this picture gives a fascinating rear-three-quarter view and well illustrates its spacious nature. With its pleasing proportions the estate had an overall length of 174.7 inches, and as much as 69 inches of length within the load space compartment. This was quite enough room to accommodate a chest of drawers, bags of animal feed and several bales of hay. Many of the estate car publicity pictures were taken on farms or stables, and these clearly indicate some of the markets at which the estate was aimed.*

PC CRESTA AND VISCOUNT 1965-1972

Although the PC range really belongs in the next part of the Vauxhall story, its inclusion in the book covering the period 1945-1964 is really quite essential, for it shows the substantial change in the range from the offerings of the post-war period. Advertised with the slogan 'The Cars For The Space Age', the new Vauxhall PC Cresta and Cresta Deluxe officially replaced the PB Cresta and Velox on 18th October 1965, a time when the Velox name was finally dropped. However, as their genesis, and most of the research and development work took place in 1964, it was felt appropriate to include the PC in this book. It was also the last variant in a long line of Vauxhall cars to carry the Cresta badge.

Whereas the PAs had seen a production figure of 173,364, the demand dropped with the PBs to 87,047, and despite a seven-year production line, the PCs would only total 60,937 when production ended in 1972. The high demand for large powerful cars was coming to an end in Britain, especially in 1967 after the Middle East conflict in June (resulting in high petrol prices), the imposition of the 70mph speed limit in July and the devaluation of the pound in the autumn.

Above: *Superior, superb, superlative, were all words that Vauxhall used to describe the new PC Cresta and PC Cresta Deluxe when it was introduced in 1965. As can be seen from the above picture it was clearly a car aimed at the businessman (or those who wanted a car of quality and comfort), and its ability for high-speed cruising mirrored this.*

The new 6-cylinder cars came to be known for the 'Coke-bottle style', so-called because of the way in which the wing line rose towards the rear in imitation of the distinctive glass bottles used for the well-known fizzy drink. It was a popular feature, and its public appeal led to Vauxhall emulating the feature on the FB Viva and the FD Victor.

The demise of the Velox meant that there were two Cresta models, the PCS being the base model, whilst the PCD was the designation for the Deluxe. Later the 140bhp Viscount would appear, but as it did not come on the scene until the summer of 1966, it is well and truly beyond the remit of this book. However, all three models shared a single body-shell and had the same mechanical layout.

The heart of the beast was the powerful 3.3 litre six-in-line engine, however this unit could be traced back quite a way, for it had originally been designed by Chevrolet to power light trucks. In its more modern form it had been used in the 1964-5 PB Velox and Cresta cars, where it brought about the unique situation of being the first Vauxhall car that was not powered by a Vauxhall-designed engine. The advantage of taking the American engine for the PB can be readily understood, when its 128bhp compared favourably against the 113bhp 2.6 engine used in the PAs and early PB s. The new engine had a cylinder bore of 92.08mm diameter and 82.55 stroke giving 3294cc. One criticism of the engine might be expressed in that it only had a four-bearing crankshaft, but otherwise it was a marvellous piece of machinery.

I can also approve the transmission, especially since the Special Tool Division of David Brown Gears at Huddersfield were involved with the prototype and later made the special gear-cutting tools for Vauxhall. Indeed, it was on a PC Cresta box that I was let loose as a young apprentice in the David Brown Training School, but shame prevents me from saying how badly I put it back together again. Having said that the gear box was a good one, the standard PC still stuck to the three-speed column change, and this link with the past really dated the car.

However, alternatives were provided as optional extras. The first of these gave an overdrive variant, operating on the top two ratios after activation by a toggle switch. The next option was a four-speed manual box with a floor-mounted column, which gave a much quicker passage through the gears. The third, and my favourite was the Powerglide automatic box, and whilst not everyone's cup of tea, it has to be admitted that this really was a superb piece of engineering. I have read some critical reports of the Powerglide, but I can do no better than echo Vauxhall's own description of what they called 'the world's best proved automatic transmission.' Indeed, it changed gear with a smoothness that could not be felt, and I did quite a lot of work with Vauxhall and the Powerglide in my days at Browns. I also know that several UK motor manufacturers secretly had the unit to bits including Rolls Royce, who (reputedly) used the Powerglide's successor, namely the General Motors Overseas Operations automatic gearbox.

If the engine and transmission had American origins, the body had a real Luton pedigree, for it was styled by David Jones ARCA. Jones had joined Vauxhall from The Royal College of Art. When he arrived in 1934, he was **the** styling department, but it was not too long before he received an assistant. By the time that the PC range was on the drawing board, a new £2.5 million Styling & Engineering Department had opened in 1964. We have to say that the styling of the PC series did much to restore 'image confidence' in the Vauxhall range, following the less than kind comments that some had made about the FB and PB series cars. In the PC range, Jones went on to produce a car style that matched the power unit and automatic transmission, and after the initial success with Cresta, Vauxhall could send out a sumptuous brochure on 20th April 1966. With this the Sales Manager (G.E. Moore) announced the arrival of a 'high prestige car which combines great refinement and luxury with a really exciting performance'. The price was £1,457 12s 11d, a snip at around £14,500 today!

Above: *Another PR shot that suggests a certain style in the six-cylinder Vauxhall, and as the BOAC pilot strides out towards a pre-production model Viscount, the suggestion is made that here is a car that accords with a certain status in life. After all, the man who 'drives' the most luxurious aircraft in the world had to have a car commensurate with his position! Didn't he?*

Below: *As this car, registered in the States Of Jersey, shows - the De-luxe Cresta had a timeless grace and elegance. David Jones' styling was right for the mid-1960s, but it still looks good today, and it would also compare favourably with any small limousine in the years between. It was a car well ahead of its time, and it worked wonders to overcome the lack-lustre appearance of the PB range that preceded it. No wonder that Ford of Great Britain found that the new Vauxhall PC cars gave very stiff competition to their MkIV range of six-cylinder cars.*

Top Left: *There is that old (rather sexist) comment that a man will trust his wife with anything except his car. Yet here we see a picture that, at first glance, reveals a trusting husband allowing his wife into the driver's seat. However, closer inspection shows it is in fact a left-hand drive Deluxe model. Despite its Swiss registration plate, this shot was taken at Gayhurst near Milton Keynes.*

Bottom Left: *The clean lines of the PC can be seen on this publicity picture which was used in a 1965 brochure to convey an image of speed. The slight blurring of the image certainly achieves this aim, but we chose this picture for the nice way in which it shows the 'Coke-bottle' styling.*

Hydraulic brakes with vacuum-servo assistance were fitted on the front wheels which had $10^{1/2}$ inch diameter discs, whilst the rear wheels used 9-inch diameter drum brakes. The wheels were usually shod (at least for the home market) with 5.90x14 tubeless cross-ply tyres, although special 7.00x14 4-ply nylon tyres were available for the driver who wanted sustained high speed motoring without the need for frequent adjustment of tyre pressures.

Externally the base Cresta was easily identified by its individual seven-inch diameter headlamps, whilst the De-luxe version sported dual headlamps of $5^{3/4}$ inch diameter. The radiator grills on the two models showed a slight difference, whilst the Deluxe also had a small and very discreet badge at the edge of the bonnet, whereas the base model just had a narrow name badge. Other small differences could be seen in the trim. Whilst both cars had bright trim around the panoramic front and rear windscreens and on the side drip rail around the windows, the Deluxe also had a fine band running along the base of the side windows which then carried on along the top of the rear wings.

Compared with the PB, the PC was a handsome-looking automobile from any perception, yet its styling was also very practical. By the clever use of curved doors and side glass, Vauxhall were able to construct a car that was a good half inch narrower than its predecessors, and at the same time give an extra four inches of width within the car saloon. Overall the PC was 69.8 inches wide, and its length was 181.8 inch on a 107.5 inch wheelbase and resulted in the PC being some 5.3 inches longer overall. This, coupled with a change in the position of the petrol tank (from over the rear axle to a position underneath the boot floor) gave a slight rise in the height of the boot. These two factors provided an increase of 16.07 cubic feet in the luggage space over the PB models, and increased the PCs to 30 cubic feet.

Further examples of Vauxhall's continued improvement were to be found in the internal specifications. To suit their limousine status, the Deluxe Crestas were given a better heater/ventilation system. This not only provided a good floor heater and screen demister, but also incorporated small grills at the outer ends of the facia panel that gave cool air distribution at face level. The floor heater directed air to each front footwell, and two more ducts directed heat into the two rear seat footwells. This heater system was also available on the base Cresta, but only as an additional cost item.

A close study of the PC will reveal how much thought had gone into its design during 1963 and 1964, and less obvious features were the high quality of sound insulation and the 44% increase in overall rigidity. 'Underfloor Comfort' (now there's a concept to think about), began to appear in Vauxhall technical literature, so it is worth briefly discussing. On the PC, Solbit Deadener spray was applied to the internal floor and transmission tunnel, and the Deluxe also had Flinkcote pads front and rear. Both models had $5/8$-inch jute felt matting covering the front and rear floor panels, with a further $3/8$-inch strip covering the transmission tunnel. A final layer of $3/8$-inch Polyether was placed on the rear floor before the carpets were fitted. On the underside of the De-luxe models floor panels, a substantive layer of under-sealant was applied.

In its seating accommodation the Cresta offered a new luxury soft fabric called Ambla on the De-luxe model, but still stuck with Vynide, which was still awful on a hot sunny day. Leather remained an optional extra on both models. The Deluxe had individual front seats as standard, but a bench seat with centre armrest was available as an extra. The base model stuck to the bench seat, but a centre armrest was again supplied as extra equipment. Both models had armrests as standard in the rear seats. The quality facia incorporated a large instrument panel, and all the standard item controls. It could also be fitted with additional equipment such as an electric clock, a built-in radio, fog lamp switch, rear window demister control, and a steering wheel lock on the ignition switch. The ten 'Magic Mirror' paint finishes for the Cresta were black, Grecian White, Storm Grey, Kestrel Grey, Meteor Blue, Pacific Blue, Cypress Green, Calypso Red, Cavalry Fawn and Jade Green. Interior colours were Calypso Red, Delta Blue, April Green and Grey Beige, in monotone finishes on the Cresta and two-tone trims on the Deluxe.

The PC concludes our look at the 20 years of Vauxhall development following the end of World War II. Our consideration of the subject has, hopefully, put this all into context and shown the progression through the years. It has not been intended as an in-depth analysis of the subject, but rather an informative over-view of the subject. It is an approach that will be followed in the other books in this series, as we cover the hundred year history of Vauxhall Motors.

The approach is a personal view from the authors, and any mistakes in the text are ours alone, but we have to emphasise that this book would not have been possible without the kind assistance of Vauxhall Motors, numerous Vauxhall enthusiasts and several Vauxhall dealers. The support of Ron Atkins and the Vauxhall Heritage Services team in developing this concept must also be recognised, for without their help, this series of books would simply not have happened.

Top Right: *Shades of things to come, with a photograph that does not really belong in a book with a time span of 1945-1964, but one which had to be included just for the sheer good looks of the new Viscount.*

Bottom Right: *Our last photograph within the body text had to be another of those 'image' pictures. This one certainly captures the luxury of the 'Space Age' car with a couple admiring a 1965 Cresta De-luxe, albeit just for the camera, but I bet they wished it was theirs!*

Acknowledgments

Above: *One of the prototype Vauxhall Viscount models based on the PC Cresta De-luxe - and with 7.025 production cars to be built, it was the shape of things to come!*

This series of books is the result of a broken-down train on the East Coast Main Line, when I was returning from a meeting at Ford's Dagenham works with a set of page proofs for an earlier book. The passenger opposite me, seeing the images on the pages I had spread out on the table, commented on their fascination before telling me he was in management at Vauxhall. I was then asked, 'had we thought of doing something on their product range?' An introduction was made, and since that time the company archivist Dennis Sherer has helped take the project along and Vauxhall have made available this wonderful collection of images for everyone to enjoy.

It has been a project that has well illustrated the pioneering technology of Vauxhall and its many capable engineers through the years. Yet it is also a tribute to the shop floor workers, the clerical staff, the dealers, and the loyal owners who have all enabled the firm to keep raising its standard. It is also dedicated to those owners who still keep the memories of Vauxhall and Bedford alive - and as the owner of four preserved Bedford coaches, I am very proud to play my own small part! **AE**

Special thanks are offered to:
John Ankerman (Chairman Vauxhall, Bedford, Opel Association)
Peter Blincow (Vauxhall Heritage Services)
Tony Burnip (former Director of Supply, Vauxhall Motors)
Ray Cooper (Senior Restorer, Vauxhall Heritage Centre)
Nigel Griggs (Vauxhall Motors)
Stuart Harris (Vauxhall Motors)
Barry Harvey (General Secretary Vauxhall 1903-57 Owners Club)
Gordon Jamieson (R. G. Jamieson, Isle of Yell)
Kerseys Garage (Vauxhall dealers Penrith)
SMT (Vauxhall dealers Scotland)
Dennis Sherer (Archivist, Vauxhall Motors)
Peter Stone (Vauxhall Motors)
Larry Sutherland (former Vauxhall dealer Lerwick)
David Turner (former senior engineer GM Holden)

A debt of gratitude is also due to the Vauxhall, Bedford, Opel Association who kindly offered to host the re-launch of this revised book at Billing Aquadrome, Northampton, in July 2001!